ARCHITECTURAL PHOTOGRAPHY
CREATIVE LARGE FORMAT

ARCHITECTURAL PHOTOGRAPHY

CREATIVE LARGE FORMAT

Urs Tillmanns

Introduction by Dr. David Meili

sinaredition

Idea: Robert Züblin
Concept: Hans-Carl Koch
Translation: Rolf Fricke
Design, layout and illustrations:
Adrian Bircher, CH-8400 Winterthur
Photo lithos: Löpfe Cliché Litho AG, CH-9434 Au/SG
Printer: Meier + Cie AG, CH-8201 Schaffhausen
Bookbinder:
Bookbindery Eibert AG, CH-8733 Eschenbach

Cover picture: Reinhart Wolf

German original title:
"Kreatives Grossformat: Architekturfotografie"
Original German edition 1993 in cooperation with
Verlag 'PHOTOGRAPHIE' AG, CH-8201 Schaffhausen

ISBN 3-7231-0035-X

Table of Contents

The Two Worlds of Architectural Photography

It is no accident that the first volume on applications in the series of "Creative Large Format" books is dedicated to architectural photography. The latter is virtually ideal for explaining the adjustments available on large format cameras, because the distracting pictorial effect of non-parallel vertical lines of a building disturbs even those viewers who are not particularly knowledgeable about photography. In schools and training centers too, architectural photographs are often used as excellent examples for achieving an understanding of the professional camera's geometry and its adjustment mechanisms.

Who are the devotees of architectural photography? The all-around photographer who, in addition to practising photojournalism, portraiture and commercial photography, also occasionally makes photographs of an impressive building, will only rarely earn the praise of the architect of that building, no matter how perfect the photographs turn out to be. The reason is that each one sees and perceives the building quite differently. The architect designed his building on the basis of certain practical specifications, whereas the photographer sees the very same building in terms of fascinating dimensions, light and shadows. Two worlds seem to confront each other: the world of the architect and the world of the photographer.

This book seeks to establish greater harmony between these two worlds. It is therefore aimed at two types of readers: One is the photographer who in addition to his current professional activities wants to concentrate on architectural photography in order to make it his specialty, and the other is the architect who has become a master of his craft and who, with a strong interest in photography, wishes to pay increasing attention to the pictorial representation of his work.

An understanding of photography as well as architecture is an absolute requirement for making expressive and technically perfect architectural photographs. The two essays that precede the representative portfolio section of this book that features internationally recognized photographers are intended to illustrate the photographic aspects and to convey an understanding of architecture.

At this point I wish to express my gratitude to the photographers whose outstanding images constitute the principal foundation of this book. I am also indebted to Hans-Carl Koch for his expertise and for his many recommendations, to David Meili for his well-founded essay on the history and nature of architecture, and to Adrian Bircher, who was responsible for the layout of this volume.

Neuhausen, September 1993   Urs Tillmanns

A good architectural photograph thrives on light and aesthetics. Aside from a few treetops in the foreground, the photographer deliberately avoided any surrounding elements and concentrated entirely on the building itself.
Photo by Reinhart Wolf, Hamburg, Germany

Architecture and Photography

"Photography is a language and the photographer is an author", writes Gabriel Bauret in an essay about the nature of photography published in 1992. The photography of architecture thus becomes a representation and an interpretation, or at least an intensive explanation in another language, by another author.

As a documentarian, the photographer supplies reproductions of architecture to architects, professionals, or to the general public. As an interpreter, he records his subjective perception of a construction project in his own medium. In the documentation as well as in the interpretation, the objectives of the client and the expected viewing habits of the target audience play a significant role. Even if the photographer takes on architecture as a personal project, without a client and not aimed at a specific audience, he still has to study the circumstances of its creation, its character and the nature of the representation of its prior interpretation.

Our overview of the interaction between architecture and photography includes a historical section, a discussion of the circumstances around the origination of architecture and an introduction to the most relevant individual subjects.

A brief History of Architectural Photography

When Nicéphore Niépce (1765 -1833) made the very first photograph in 1826, he unintentionally made the very first architectural photograph as well. To this day it is the oldest document from the infancy of photography, and on it one can clearly recognize the contours of two buildings that were located across from Niépce's study. Niépce merely wanted to record something in a natural way using a mechanical device, and the view from his window was the nearest convenient subject. This legendary image already contains a major characteristic of an architectural photograph: a representation of perspective. In spite of its static nature and its planes, the photograph conveys something unreal. The very long exposure time resulted in an unnatural distribution of light and shadows. The sun is shining on both sides of the roof at the same time.

The depiction of architecture, next to the portraiture of persons, was one of the primary needs for early photography. Architectural draftsmen and painters began using the Camera Obscura during the Renaissance to make their task easier while drawing a view of a city.

Like portrait photography, architectural photography also dates back to Louis-Jacques Mandé Daguerre (1787-1851). His first photographs of street scenes were made in 1839, and for practical reasons, just like Niépce, he took them from a window in his study. With the recording of exterior views with the Daguerreotype, this new medium was able to penetrate a domain hitherto reserved for drawing and its related reproduction techniques. During the 19th century, there was a virtually insatiable interest in Europe and in North America for historical monuments of foreign countries, people and eras. The Daguerreotype was used for archaeological photography as early as 1840, and already in 1841 the first album of the most famous monuments in the world was introduced in Paris!

With the emergence of the Calotype, the range of applications for photography as a means of documentation expanded significantly. Some of the first Calotypes made by William Henry Fox Talbot (1800-1877) show architectural renditions with a nearly classic character. In 1846 Fox Talbot photographed the Royal Pavilion in Brighton. Then came a series of architectural photographs, which technologically and stylistically established the medium of photography in the world of applied arts. Six years later, after the World Exposition in London,

Nicéphore Niépce (1765-1833): View from his study (1826). The first preserved photograph and also the first architectural photograph. From the Gernsheim Collection at the University of Texas in Austin, USA.

photographer Philip Henry Delamotte (1820-1889), who was originally from France, presented one of the very first architectural reports. It documented the disassembly, the moving and the re-erection of the buiding that was to have the greatest influence on the architecture of the second half of the 19th century: the Crystal Palace of Joseph Paxton.

From the Classics to Pictorialism

It is interesting to note that during the second half of the 19th century, conservative architecture was photographed strictly conservatively. Up until it began to flourish after the first world war, architectural photography was cumbersome and static. Its stylistic evolution often seemed to lag more than a generation behind painting. But the buildings that were being erected for residences and for world cities hardly justified a different interpretation. These early architectural photographs are characterized by a central perspective, strong symmetry and good modelling of structural elements with light, but there is hardly any personal style that can be recognized.

A turning point in the evolution of architecture and architectural photography was the construction of the Eiffel Tower in the year 1889. Numerous photographers, some on official assignments, others working on speculation, recorded the stages of construction of the tower and informed the world at large. All of their photographs are thoroughly static, influenced by classic concepts of rendering. A few years ago, an album was discovered in Paris, assembled by an unknown amateur who showed this event in a totally different manner, with the direct inclusion of project workers and capturing the atmosphere of the construction site. That document, much more modern by today's viewing habits, proves how professional photography of the period was bound by aesthetics, technique, and by its concessions to public tastes.

The crisis in photography was taking place not only in architectural reproduction. A new generation of photographers rebelled against the starchy rules, which also governed portrait and landscape photography, seeking more individual styles of expression. The origins and beginnings of this subjective, painterly style direction, which today's topical literature refers to as pictorialism, cannot be traced back to a particular name, nor to a definite subject.

However there are similarities to be found in the publications media and in the target audiences. The preferred products were postcards and illustrated magazines, and the preferred public was the young adult citizens of large metropolitan cities. For the first time, the medium also catered to the tastes of women.

In Europe, pictorialists showed little interest in architectural subjects. Only in England did the tradition of employing elements of gothic architecture continue, either for embellishment or as primary subjects for still-lifes.

In Central Europe at the end of the 19th century, a naturalism strongly influenced by contemporary painting is not clearly differentiated from pictorialism. The outstanding exponent of this genre is Eugène Atget (1857-1927). He began to document Paris other than by its great monuments, and he perceived photography as an aid, as a foundation for the contemporary paintings of impressionism. Atget, who was extraordinarily productive, and

Frédéric Boissonas (1858-1946): The Parthenon, circa 1905. The Boissonas photographic dynasty of Geneva in Switzerland specialized in the production of high quality picture books with architectural, landscape and art illustrations. Using tall tripods, Boissonas achieved camera positions that produced perspectives similar to those on an elevation drawing.

whose style subtly evolved over a long period of time, exerted a major influence, even after his death, on photography of daily life in American cities. So much so that American photographer Berenice Abbott (1898-1991) not only became a promoter of his work on the new continent, she also patterned her own personal style largely on the example set by Atget.

Characteristic of American architectural photography at the end of the 19th century is its uncomplicated relationship to the architecture of the present. The environment of buildings at the doorsteps of Alfred Stieglitz

Eugène Atget was a pioneer in naturalism whose city views of Paris introduced an entirely new style of architectural photograph. Photo: Collection of the Musée de l'Elysée, Lausanne, CH

(1864-1946) and Edward Steichen (1879-1973) as a matter of course served them as scenery. With such a relationship to reality, American photography was able to establish a direct dialog with architecture. Architects and photographers began to see with the same eyes.

New Functionalism and Subjectivity

Because they do not conform to conventional seeing habits, futurism and surrealism are styles that are difficult to classify in the traditional description of the history of photography. The significance of futurism in the evolution of architectural photography and of architecture itself tends to be underestimated.

In reaction to the challenges posed by emerging modern technologies, the German Werkbund was founded in 1907, and in 1919, architect Walter Gropius led the founding of the Bauhaus in Weimar, Germany. The objective of the new movement was a synergy between art, trades and industry. Architecture was favored in the practical implementation of this objective, because it fosters a direct confluence of all the creative forces. Since photography

was also regarded as an ideal combination of craftsmanship, technical progress and artistic expression, architectural photography occupies a relevant position in the cultural heritage of this endeavor.

The photographic activities of the Bauhaus took place during the decade from 1920 to 1930. But it was only towards the end of that period that photography was taught as a separate subject. The initiator and most prominent practitioner of the style that came to be known as "The New Functionality" (from the German "Die Neue Sachlichkeit") is considered to be Albert Renger-Patzsch (1897-1966). Characteristic of the "new functionalism" is the emphasis on diagonals in the composition of the photographs. This in turn imparts a dynamic to architectural photographs that can be enhanced even further by the use of unconventional camera positions. Another influence is the aesthetics derived from graphic techniques and their possibilities in representation. Black-and-white photographs often seem harsh, they show deep shadows contrasted by highlights. Architecture is often perceived as somewhat abstract and planar.

The rigid perception of photographic aesthetics was already being challenged by Renger-Patzsch' contemporaries, who were also active at the Bauhaus. The evolution of the architectural photographs of Andreas Feininger and Laszlo Moholy-Nagy (1895-1946), was soon permeated again by naturalistic and pictorial elements. Werner Mantz (1901-1986), who achieved a technical as well as an aesthetic proficiency in the photography of interiors, used light as a creative element. He began to prefer the mood of night time for his exterior photographs, which enabled him to achieve dramatic interpretations of buildings and structures.

Bauhaus photographers also influenced the evolution of architectural photography in America, as Atget did during the previous generation. Young photographers dis-

Otto Rietmann (1846-1942). Construction of the Goetheanum in Dornach (1914). The photograph shows the interesting design of the building, which was destroyed by a fire a few years later.

covered the rural architecture of the midwest. Clapboard walls, shingled roofs, corrugated iron all have graphic structures that lend themselves effectively for black-and-white photography. Walker Evans (1903-1975) is among the best known photographers of rural architecture. He combined static architectural with social documentary photographs, which he, along with other male and female photographers, produced for the American Farm Security Administration (FSA) after 1937.

While the creative arts in Europe used photographs mostly for collages, quite a different trend, based directly on a photographic way of seeing, evolved in American paintings during the thirties. Painters like Charles Scheeler (1883-1965) and Edward Hopper (1882-1967) produced oil paintings which could be identified as paintings only after close inspection. Their hyper-realism interprets situations that viewers had already experienced "photographically". But in doing so, neither Sheeler nor Hopper were questioning the possibilities of photography as a medium for artistic expression. Painting offered them technical means that photography could not yet match in the thirties and forties. Sheeler worked with strongly differentiated colors, while Hopper mixed different light sources with resulting contrasts that no photographic film available that time could have accommodated.

With ominous political changes and the emigration of intellectuals as well as of the photographic avant-garde, the "new functionalism" style underwent hardly any further development in Germany. On the other hand, big city photography gave fresh impulses to a new kind of photography that involved men and women as inhabitants, users and creators of architecture. Photographers like André Kertész (1894-1985), who worked in Paris and later emigrated to the United States, transformed subjective experiences into photographic images. After some experimentation with photomontages and after intensive scrutiny of the work of experimental artists like Man Ray (1890-1976), they turned to photojournalism. Highly portable and fast 35 mm cameras fostered the tendency towards subjectivity. Within that generation of photographers, which included Henri Cartier-Bresson (born 1908), Brassai (1899-1976) and Robert Doisneau (born 1912), Architecture was but one of many themes that were always portrayed in relation to man. It is typical of that genre of photography that it no longer sought to convey merely the straight content of a photograph to a broad public, but also its specifically photographic interpretation and view.

Postwar Trends

With the predominance of photojournalism and the changes it caused in viewing habits, traditional architectural photography became more of a practical type of photography that was not considered to have any artistic or possibly intellectual components. Architectural, industrial and commercial photographers were still thought of as craftsmen. Their market was advertising, trade publications and archives. The requirements were technical precision, as objective or – in the case of advertisements – as embellished a depiction as possible. If one compares the style of architectural photography up to the mid-sixties with present trends, one notices a distinct change from a practical to an artistic interpretation. We would like to describe two factors that influenced this evolution.

With the appearance of photographic galleries, a new market came into being after 1970 in Europe as well for a type of photography that could cultivate artistic objectives. Particularly photographers who, influenced by the Americans, began to take an interest in large format photography and chose architecture in addition to landscapes as their range of subjects. Related to the activities in the galleries is a lively production of art books, which also promoted artistically oriented architectural photography. As in the 19th century, there are two predominant subjects: a pictorial representation of architecture in foreign countries, particularly in North America and Southeast Asia, and the discovery of one's own national architectural he-

This photograph by H.G. Esch, Cologne, Germany, dramatically documents how transient architecture can be. Esch used an extremely long focal length to make this photograph.

ritage. Decaying industrial architecture seemed to have a special attraction for large format photographers.

A different evolution took place in industrial photography. Illustrated annual reports, calendars and company brochures became the equivalent of business cards for corporations. While large companies in America started to employ photographers to illustrate their annual reports and presentations in the forties, in Central Europe and Japan this market for creative photography only opened up during the sixties.

The most important fields of application for architectural photography, the depiction of buildings for architects, contractors, trade publications and trade press up until a few years ago offered hardly any opportunities for creative composition. In Italy however, a new kind of architectural publication emerged which combined form and content into a visual expression. A new kind of architectural photography began to flourish in this environment, which became an active and dedicated part of the creative process.

Photography as Part of the Working Process

An architect thinks in terms of images. He lives and works with knowledge gleaned from buildings he has already seen and experienced. From that he develops visions of rooms and structures that will evolve through various stages until they become a reality.

An architect's work is certainly not a lonesome activity. It is supported by many other individuals who perform functions related to a project. In addition, the construction assignment, the volume and the basic formal design of a building is largely determined by external factors.

The architect and his team are in the center of communication processes. They exchange ideas, concepts and findings among clients, co-designers such as engineers and planners, builders and also the financers. Many concepts can only be communicated by means of visual media. The means of communication are drawings, plans, models, and photographs.

Applications of Photography

Work on a new project starts with an idea, which is first put on paper in the form of a sketch. The draft constitutes the starting point for developing detailed plans and as the next step, the execution plans. These are followed by construction and documentation of the finished building.

Most of the phases of this working process take place on paper. In order to explore areas for the application of photography, one has to differentiate between activities that are aimed at the realization of the project and those that, looking back, are intended for the documentation of said project. There is a close connection between documentation and planning. Architecture is in a continuous process of evolution which again and again starts from something that already exists.

Photography offers no alternatives to drawings for suggested layouts, planning and designing. After all, the camera can only record existing buildings or models. The conversion of ideas and concepts into pictures is left to drawings. Photography is also unsuitable for the preparation of execution plans. Wherever dimensions are used, it is not sufficiently precise.

The most important applications of architectural photography occur before and after the actual work of the architect. During the preparation of a construction project, it serves to document existing buildings and their elements. For comparison purposes, the architect procures images from his personal files, from trade literature, or he makes his own photographs. Since the quality of photographs needed for this purpose is not critical, instant pictures or even amateur camcorders are often used. Greater demands are placed on the photographic documentation of the construction site and of a housing project development area. Specific sections of such photographs, with their perspectives corrected, are needed for photographic presentations.

During the planning and the construction phases of a building project, three interesting opportunities offer themselves to profesional photographers. They can be considered as specialized fields within architectural photography, and they cover the photographic recording of mock-ups, documenting the progress of construction, and photographic surveys of the building site. In all three tasks is the photographer confronted directly with the working domain of the architect.

The design phase is concluded with an architectural model, intended to help the owners, the authorities and the public visualize what the finished building might look like. The impression created by a photograph of the model is often more persuasive than that of the three-dimensional model itself. The photographer selects an angle and careful lighting that simulate the future setting of the building. Good model photographs can contribute significantly to a positive impression of the construction project on the authorities and the public, they may even be a decisive factor. Until the completion of the building, photographs of the model are also used for press releases.

The technical documentation of the construction phase is often neglected. It is basically wise to make photographic records of all the important stages during their execution. Photographs of construction elements and building components that later will no longer be accessible are particularly important.

It is in the interest of construction management and participating investors that these photographs be made in such a way that they will be useful in documenting and in resolving possible claims for construction damage and later on in preparing remodelling plans. Photographs are especially valuable documents in case the execution deviates from the original plans.

Complementing the technical documentation, an additional coverage can be made of human, entrepreneurial and craftsmanship aspects. Photography fills important

Photographs of mock-ups are important to the architect during the design phase. The direction of the light should correspond to the natural position of the sun. In addition to overall views, pictures from the perspective of a pedestrian are also called for. Photos by Rolf Wessendorf, Schaffhausen, Switzerland.

psychological needs. It promotes the identification of all the participants with the project, thus enhancing the working climate. Construction boss, architect, and workers will have pictures that document their achievements in a more pleasing way than the finished building.

Photographic coverage of a large construction job is both an artistic as well as a technical challenge. To the people who appear in the photographs it is more important than the surrounding architecture and technology that they be recognizable, not in the way the photographer sees them, but as they themselves wish to be seen in their working environment. Good opportunities for photographic coverage are customary events that punctuate a construction job, like groundbreaking, topping-off ceremonies, or the break-through of a tunnel. Most of the photographic reports of construction jobs that entered the history of photography consist of staged photographs. Managed photographs of working procedures give those who are involved the opportunity to present themselves. Their documentary value is therefore often greater than that of a spontaneous snapshot.

The most important phase of the photographer's job comes after the construction project has been completed: assembly of the pictorial documentation. For the architect it represents a stock-taking of the finished project; for the owner it is an overview of the building before or at the beginning of its utilization. These pictures should also be suitable for publications and for advertising.

Diverse requirements often result in the need for separate photographic assignments to ensure that all aspects are covered. Technical problems can occur when a photographic record is to be made of rooms before equipment is installed or before they are occupied. Often construction can only be completed after equipment has been installed or after the premises are already in use.

The most important Techniques of Representation

As late as the fifties, freehand sketching was a required subject in most of the technical colleges where architecture was taught. The first field trips for aspiring architects led to medieval guildhalls and cathedral squares and to antique ruins. The sketchbooks made during the student days often became the most important aids in later design work. Architectural drawings, recognized as a distinct art form since the renaissance, were an important element in academic education.

Even though photography has a firm place in architectural design offices, architects think and work with graphic means of expression. Renderings are based directly on basic drawing patterns and conventions. Because of their characteristics, some of them, like sections, floorplans and location specifications, cannot be generated photographically or be replaced by photographs.

The simplest and most used representation is the elevation. The upright portion of a building is rendered in terms of a vertical plane. As a rule, only façades can be depicted in elevations. Elements with depth, like a slanted roof, are shown in a foreshortened form. A photograph is equally as appropriate as a drawing for showing the elevation of a building. In drawings, there is the concern for precision and accuracy of details, while in photography distortion and shadow detail become critical factors. It is easy for the person making a drawing to select an imaginary viewpoint in the center of a vertical plane. A photographer, on the other hand, would need a significantly raised camera position or at least an adjustable professional camera. Detail rendition is largely dependent on lighting. In a drawing, shadows are used for effects partly intended to appeal to the viewer on an emotional level. In photography, when the texture of the façade is emphasized by grazing light, this may result in an unwanted dramatization. This problem constantly led to experimentation in the enlarging of the photographs. By raising the contrast of prints of façades with simple structures and few details, their impact can come close that of an elevation drawing. For detail-rich, very ornate façades, however, such as those found in baroque literature, detailed drawings remain superior to photographic renditions.

The classic form of representation in architectural drawing is the perspective. This term is derived from the Latin ars perspectiva, the art of looking through. The discovery and the development of perspective representation is one of the great achievements of the Italian renaissance. In architectural representation, the perspective is of particular importance because it makes it possible to visualize rooms that do not yet exist. The starting point for a perspective drawing is the image plane. That is the theoretical plane on to which the three-dimensional building is to be projected as it is seen by the eye.

Thus a drawing is like a back to front photographic process. While architectural photography depicts rooms and, by means of perspective enables the viewer to perceive their space, drawings use it to reconstruct rooms on plane surfaces. The image plane is to a perspective architectural drawing what the film plane is to a camera.

As a rule, the draftsman or the draftswoman begins with the horizon line, which is intended to represent eye level. If it is shifted above normal human eye level, a bird's-eye view results. A lower viewpoint makes the subject grow to monumental heights. In particular symmetrical building structures, staircases and interior rooms are rendered with a central perspective by the designer. The vanishing point in this case is located in the center of the picture.

The advanced school of perspective rendition shows the superiority of drawings over photography. When it comes to depicting buildings and spatial situations with several vanishing points, the photographer will encounter

Highrise building "zur Palme", Zurich, Switzerland (1964). Overall view and main façade. Example of the objectivity-oriented architectural photography style of the fities and sixties. Photos by Walter Binder (born 1931), Zurich, Switzerland

theoretical limits. In this case, the domain of the draftsman begins not only at the design stage, but it also includes the documentation of existing structures.

The advanced school of architectural drawing includes *axonometry* and *isometry*. Isometry and axonometry are equivalent terms. Isometry involves overall views of architectural situations, whereas axonometry applies to individual structural units.

Unlike a perspective drawing, isometry is true to scale. Lines and planes remain parallel. Pure Isometry has no vanishing points nor foreshortenings. This creates the impression that the depicted objects grow larger toward the rear and downward. Shortened Isometry seeks to approach human perception characteristics by using different scales along the three axis.

Isometric representations can be accomplished with adjustable professional cameras. The shortened isometry mode especially, is of interest to photography. In this case, however, photography would not provide measurable precision. The latter is still a primary objective of photogrametric photography and evaluation.

For perspective as well as for isometric rendition, the draftsman has to define the distance from the image plane. This determines the subtended angle of view with which the object is seen. Instruction manuals on architectural drawing cite an optimal viewing angle of approximately 60 degrees. The greater the viewing angle, the more difficult the alignment with the vanishing point. In this situation, the eye and the camera are far more efficient than a drawing, both being able to accommodate larger picture elements.

The Photographer and the Architect in Dialog

As decision processes become more complex, communication among the participants becomes even more important. Successful cooperation between an architect and a photographer requires not only a realistic understanding of the application possibilities for photography, but also a common language.

Architecture and and photography are artistically oriented forms of expression with many aspects in common. Both have to deal with the tension between functionality and cultural aspirations. As a rule, both the photographer as well as the architect have to subordinate their creativity to pragmatic objectives. There are differences in dealing with pictures and spatial concepts. A photographer is used to reducing spaces to planes. The architect has the task of creating spaces and three-dimensional structures. The photographer furthermore does not just want to record reality, he also wants to interpret it. That interpretation changes and manipulates the architecture.

The attitude of architects toward photography is ambivalent. Often personal inclinations may have been the determining factor when an architect reached for a camera. It is known that Eero Saarinen (1910-1961) was an enthusiastic 35 mm photographer and that Frank Lloyd Wright (1869-1959) too, often used a camera. Le Corbusier, who also became part of modern history of art as a painter, was rather skeptical about photographic documentation of his buildings. Quite a few architects changed profession to become photographers, especially during the worldwide depression or while in exile.

That hardly points up differences in the visual language of photographers and architects. Communication problems occur only when the assignment has not been understood correctly and when insufficient consideration has been given to the architect's intentions. The evaluation of architectural photography by an architect is based on a criterion that is different from that of a photographic critic. The architect basically wants to derive as much information as possible from a photograph. He is also interested in making it possible for a viewer to visualize and to experience a building in three dimensions. In the process, it is quite desirable to convey the building's ambiance as well. There is less of a need for an interpretation of the depicted building by the photographer. Unconventional angles of view and unusual lighting compromise the information content as much as abstractions do.

Often photographs are used only as supplements to drawings and plans. A comparison between a drawing and the corresponding photograph becomes easier when the perspective has been corrected. If the architect presented his work in an isometric rendition, a related photograph with too strong a perspective may be disconcerting. This becomes difficult when the setting permits a total photographic overview only with a very large viewing angle. The best alternative is to divide it into a series of partial views using viewpoints and viewing angles matched to human perception. In addition to perspective, which can be controlled with skilled work and good technical aids, experience shows that lighting is the cause of most of the problems. The photographer uses light to create structures, whereas the architect uses it mainly to create moods. The architectural effect of building details and façades changes with the position of the sun. Only a few buildings make a good impression in direct light with harsh shadows. Diffuse light makes façades with large glass- or metal surfaces have a softer look and finer textures. In this regard it is wise to ask the architect or the client to indicate the desired effect. It continues to be up to the photographer to discover new qualities of architecture by making his photographs at unusual times of the day.

Other problems present themselves during the photographic documentation of building interiors. In large modern building projects, lighting is a pertinent creative ele-

While architects as a rule require overall views for the documentation and for advertising purposes...

a steel contractor prefers detail views that clearly emphasize his type of work. Photos by Chris Gascoigne, London, GB

ment that must not be indiscriminately altered by the use of additional light sources. If the available light is inadequate for photography, it is customary in traditional architectural photography to attempt to reinforce the existing light sources. This method is obviously unpractical in the halls of a shopping center. If the limits of high speed films, exposure times, and lens speeds are reached, here too it becomes essential to discuss the priorities for the photograph with the client. In exceptional situations it can be quite appropriate to replace the photographs with perspective drawings.

Architecture never functions in isolation. Correlation with nearby buildings, housing development situations and adjacent terrain is as much a part of the creative task as is the building project itself. The surroundings and the scale of building projects therefore merit special attention. For the documentation to be as objective as possible, it is desirable that buildings be depicted in the same way the viewer would see them. Extreme camera positions and angles of view may be interesting photographically, but they are hardly likely to communicate the architect's intentions properly.

Only a few photographers enjoy the opportunity of being allowed to work on projects in which the building assignment, the creative possibilities and the personality of the architect stand out above the conventional. As a rule, architectural photography also requires an understanding of everyday culture. Here there are few common traits. In most cases, buildings are based on industrially prefabricated elements, from the facings of façades to staircase railings. The challenge to the photographer must not be the interpretation of a building. Presumably the architect and the building sponsors will indicate the wish to have their project shown to its best advantage,

and depending on the intended uses of the pictures, posterization techniques may be appropriate. The more ordinary a building's appearance, the greater is the weighting placed on its furnishings and surroundings. Additions such as papier-mâché trees, hedges and cars are used already at the architectural model stage as indispensable aids to simulate an attractive setting. Unfortunately, at the completion of construction, trees and landscaping are often only just being started. If people and vehicles are included to add life to the photographs, one has to remember that trends and fashions change fairly fast, so that the usefulness of such photographs is also short-lived. This aspect should also be brought to the attention of the client.

Architecture in Images

Architecture is a photographic subject that has to relate directly to the craftsmanship and artistic performance of those who have created the object to be depicted. The photograph is a synthesis of their own concept and the visual impression that the architect and the master builder convey with their work.

As early as in the 18th century, theories were formulated as to whether buildings of distinct style periods should also be represented in specific styles of drawing. In this vein, a unique style emerged for the representation of antique ruins. This question was pertinent mostly in the

19th century and its architecture, on which nearly all European and non-European styles had an influence. Modern architectural photography too, has numerous possibilities of expression, which are applied consciously or unconsciously in the depiction of the different types and appearances of buildings. A prerequisite for the judicious application of these possibilities is a basic knowledge of the history of architecture.

Architectural Styles – Photographic Styles

The history of European architecture cannot be summarized in just a few periods. We will limit ourselves to a discussion of those aspects that are helpful for an understanding of the relationship between architectural and photographic styles. Every construction project and every architectural situation has its own character, which is determined by its origination and its utilization. For an in-depth photographic coverage, it is indispensable to become familiar with the individual history of a building project. In order to understand its current appearance, one also needs information about its utilization and about modifications that may have been made.

A distinctive characteristic of European Architecture is its lasting concern with its own history. The languages of forms and shapes of earlier periods are constantly being taken into consideration and architectural achievements of the past are constantly being reinterpreted. In this context, the highest significance is attached to the understanding of the architecture of classical antiquity. The Italian renaissance was influenced by Roman and Greek building styles, creating the foundations for evolutionary trends that continue into the present. Influenced by the renaissance, and thus indirectly by classic antiquity, is baroque architecture, which characterizes nearly all major European cities. The very same traditions are revived in the concern for history in the 19th century and in the monumental architecture of the 20th century. Their latest offshoots are the tendencies of the present that have been termed "postmodern".

Most of the buildings with these historical styles pose similar problems to the photographer. As a rule they – castles, palaces and ecclesiastical buildings – have great volume, present monumental façades and have a symmetrical design. Many of these buildings were conceived to become an imposing sight from a distance, set in spacious surroundings. Because of neighboring buildings that were erected at a later time, their original exterior splendor is often hardly recognizable and difficult to recreate on film. Buildings in the classical style elicit a static impression. This interpretation not always does justice to historical reality. Particularly in the baroque period and in

the 19th century, architecture served mainly as a background setting for a colorful social life. Historical depictions of buildings that show their utilization are quite revealing. A handy access to historical illustrations and to the history of construction is provided by cultural and travel guides.

Medieval and medieval-looking structures are best photographed with a romantic look. Pictorialists of the 19th century already preferred romantic moods created by subtle lighting and soft-focus effects to depict English Gothic Revival. Today these buildings often lack the appropriate surroundings to project their original grandeur. In converting this language of forms into photographs, many architectural photographers emulate puristic historical preservationists who prefer to view historical buildings in as functional and sober a context as possible. Totally different possibilities are demonstrated by directors of historical motion pictures, such as Lucino Visconti, who succeeded in recreating the thriving atmosphere of such buildings by means of befitting decoration and enlivenment.

Approximately twice as many buildings were erected in Europe and in North America between 1850 and 1914 as there were during several preceding centuries. Several times as many buildings again were constructed

The Cathedral of Reims in France. Even in the 20th century, art historical works are among the most frequent applications of architectural photography. Photo by Martin Hürlimann (1897-1984).

Geographic Information System for the old town section of Freiburg in Switzerland. The technical breakthrough in the field of electronic image manipulation created a new market for architectural photography. Photo courtesy of Unisys AG, Switzerland

photograph, he is entitled to protection of his images from modifications. With the avalanche of photographs that are manipulated and produced by electronic image management systems, copyrights are frequently neglected. Architectural photographs in particular, can serve as attractive backgrounds in advertising photographs and for product presentations. "Architecture" is a frequently selected category in commercial picture agencies. The capabilities of electronic image management also open a new market for photographers: the production of largely impersonal and therefore widely usable background pictures. Thus the photographer performs a function in the world of electronic image management that is comparable to that of the backdrop painter in the early days of the daguerreotype.

In spite of these critical objections, electronic image management has launched a new chapter in the history of architectural photography. The borderline betwen the type of photography that faithfully reflects reality and that which produces pictures has become blurred. Exposed to a flood of visual impressions, the eye can now hardly distinguish a true reproduction from an artificially generated picture. With the new viewing habits, the expectations of the viewer and the challenges to photography have grown considerably.

Dr. David Meili

technique often eliminates the need for a laborious drawing rendition of the subject on site. It is not, however, capable of producing scaled plans by mechanical means.

Electronic image manipulation also creates copyright problems for the photographer. If he can prove that his creative ideas were instrumental in the composition of the

Architectural Styles and Representative Buildings

Architectural Style	Characteristic Features	Some Typical and Often Photographed Styles
Egyptian Architecture	**Squares, equilateral triangles and trapezoids as creative features, massive columns and heavy blocks**	**Cheops Pyramid (4600 B.C.)** **Temples of Luxor and Thebes (1400 B.C.)**
Greek Architecture	**Symmetry, carefully calculated proportions, Ionic and Doric columns**	**Acropolis in Athens (circa 420 B.C.)** **Theater of Epidaurus (circa 350 B.C.)** **Temple of Paestum (circa 300 B.C.)**
Roman Architecture	**Adoption of Greek style elements, monumental functional buildings**	**Colosseum in Rome (A.D. 70-82)** **Pompeii (destroyed A.D. 79)** **Caracalla-Baths in Rome (A.D. 211-217)** **Pont du Gard (southern France)**
Byzantine Architecture	**Extended naves in churches, round domes, brick walls, fresco paintings, mosaics**	**Hagia Sophia in Istanbul (circa A.D. 560)** **San Vitale in Ravenna (6th century)**
Roman Architecture	**Round columns and arched vaults**	**Cathedral in Worms (10th century)** **Convent church in St. Etienne (circa 1070)** **Cathedral and Leaning Tower of Pisa (circa 1170)**
Gothic Architecture	**Pointed arches, tracery, rosettes, braced exterior walls**	**Notre Dame Cathedral, Paris (12th - 14th century)** **Chartres Cathedral (13th century)** **Strassbourg Cathedral (13th - 19th century)** **City of Carcassonne, southern France (13th - 19th century)** **St. Vith's Cathedral in Prague (14th century)**

Architectural Styles and Representative Buildings

Architectural Style	Characteristic Features	Some Typical and Often Photographed Styles
Islamic Architecture	**Brick structures plastered with loam, massive buildings, round domes, rigorous ornamental art, mosaics**	**Mosque in Damascus (8th century)** **Ibn Tulun Mosque in Cairo (9th century)** **Isfahan in Iran (circa 1000)** **Alhambra in Granada (13th century)**
Chinese Architecture	**Single-story buildings, modular construction, loam or wood as building materials**	**Great Wall of China (begun 5th century B.C.)** **Sung Tuan Temple in Honan (A.D. 523)** **Forbidden City in Beijing (mostly 17th century)**
Japanese Architecture	**Axially symmetric designs, many variations, light wood construction**	**Temple in Kyoto (14th - 17th century)**
Italian Renaissance	**Adoption of Roman and Greek style elements, early construction rather cumbersome, later freer and elegant domed buildings, decoration with statuary**	**Cathedral in Florence (after 1420)** **St. Peter's Cathedral in Rome (15th and 16th century)** **Villa Rotunda of Palladio in Vicenza (1550)**
Middle- and northern European Renaissance	**Incorporation of gothic traditions, monumental castles and palaces**	**Palace of Fontainebleau (circa 1530)** **Louvre in Paris (circa 1550)** **Escorial in Madrid (16th century)** **Wollaston Hall in Nottingham (circa 1580)** **Guildhouses in Amsterdam and Leiden (16th cent.)**
Baroque Architecture	**Dynamic chambers and façades, undulating walls, classic architectural details in free arrangements**	**San Carlo in Rome (circa 1630)** **St. Paul's Cathedral in London (circa 1670)** **Bishopric in Melk (circa 1690)** **Zwinger in Dresden (circa 1720)** **Versailles (circa 1700)**
Classicism and Historicism	**Return to classic building structures and form language, incorporation of medieval and other styles, including non-European ones**	**Pantheon in Paris (circa 1740)** **Pavillion in Brighton (circa 1780)** **Glyptothel in Munich (1860-1830)** **Schauspielhaus in Berlin (1818-1824)**
Industrial Architecture of the 19th century	**New construction techniques resulting in new spatial structures, exposed metal construction**	**Iron Bridge in Derby (1779)** **Gare de l'Est in Paris (1847)** **Galleria Vitorio Emanuele II in Milan (1867)** **Eiffel Tower in Paris (1889)**
Art Nouveau and Art Deco	**Free forms, departure from existing conventions, emphasis on decoration and artistic craftsmanship**	**Sagrada Familia Cathedral in Barcelona (ca. 1900)** **Metro in Paris (circa 1900)** **Woolworth Building in New York City (1913)**
Bauhaus and Functionalism, Modernism	**Function can be recognized from the form, modular construction of concrete and glass**	**Steiner House in Vienna (1909)** **Villa Savoie in Poissy (Le Corbusier 1925)** **Bauhaus in Dessau (1925)** **Town house in Hilversum (1926)** **Falling Water house (Frank Lloyd Wright 1933)**
Urban Architecture of the 20th century		**Unité d'Habitation, Marseille (Le Corbusier 1946)** **Brasilia (after 1950)** **World Trade Center in New York City (1970)**
High Tech and Postmodernism		**Centre Pompidou in Paris (1972)** **Sears Tower in Chicago (1980)** **Lloyd's of London (1986)** **Institute du Monde Arabe in Paris (1988)**

The Tools

Architectural Photography places high demands on the photographer. On one hand he must have enough intuitive power and sufficient knowledge of architecture to be able to discuss the assignment with his client – usually the architect – and to understand the relevant architectural aspects of the building to be photographed. On the other hand – unlike many other fields of photographic coverage – architectural photography cannot be performed with just any camera. The demands on the equipment are extraordinarily high, as we will note right away.

Fortunately the equipment array for architectural photography is limited to an appropriate camera outfit (see Volume 1: Basics and Applications, Chapter 7.6 and the Appendix in the present Volume). Extensive lighting equipment and a fully equipped studio, which would be prerequisite number one for many types of commercial photography, are generally not necessary, unless one also specializes in the photography of interior architecture or of architectural models in addition to the primary exterior photography. Nevertheless there are certain items of equipment for exterior photography that must not be overlooked.

Without a doubt, the most important one is the tripod – or tripods. An architectural photographer will usually own several tripods, among them an especially heavy one that can readily support an 8 x 10" professional camera without any vibrations. There is one important factor in architectural and landscape photography that is easily underestimated: vibrations caused by wind. Even though we often assume in practice that the tripod being used is adequate for the camera being employed, the photographs frequently still show mysterious unsharpnesses. In many cases, the wind played an unexpected role, because a large format camera presents a not-to-be underestimated surface to the wind. The only defense is a particularly heavy tripod construction.

A second tripod, more in the lightweight category, is always helpful when the photographer has to select a camera position that is not right next to the parking lot, or when he has to carry his outfit for a distance or when he has to climb several flights of stairs (unfortunately, elevators may often not be available). Such a lightweight or secondary tripod still has to be sufficiently rigid to support a 4 x 5" professional camera without any vibrations. It would obviously be the more portable of the two tripods mentioned above, with a convenient tripod head, so that swings and tilts can readily be set on other cameras as well. In extreme cases, this tripod head should be able to pan easily, so that it could be used with a video camera, because it is not at all far-fetched for the photographer to offer and furnish his client a videotape along with the purely photographic coverage, for instance showing the various stages of construction of a building in an electronic motion picture mode as well. The longer the tape, the more assignments for such combined coverage will the photographer receive from his clients.

Under certain circumstances, for example when lenses with very long focal lengths are being used, it may be necessary to support the rail unit with two tripods. Reinhart Wolf used this technique to make his sensational pictures of the tops of New York skyscrapers, thus adding a new style to architectural photography.

In addition to the tripod, a reliable portable light meter for incident and reflected light measurements also belongs in the photographer's gadget bag. In particular with

An architectural photographer must not only master the technique, he must also be familiar with the subject of architecture itself in order to produce characteristic images of the building style or the architect's ideas. Photo: H.G. Esch, Cologne, Germany.

its new Expolux Measurement and Shutter System, Sinar offers an optimal system, which not only measures the light at the film plane, but which is also capable of taking the lighting contrast into account. Especially versatile too, is the Booster-1 unit in conjunction with a Minolta Exposure Meter III, IV or IV F *(see Volume 1: Basics and Applications, Chapter 5.2)*, a combination that not only permits precise readings at the film plane, but which can also be used as a convenient manual exposure meter. Photographers prefer a portable exposure meter for certain photographic situations, especially in conjunction with a lightweight and compact equipment outfit. It is also useful for advance evaluation of the assignment, to obtain an initial assessment of the prevailing lighting conditions.

An important role falls to the observation of the ground glass screen. There are several aids to shield the screen effectively from stray light in a bright daylight environment, which are explained in greater detail in the *sections under 1.2 of Volume 1: Basics and Applications*. The lens must also be shielded from stray light during the exposure itself, by means of a properly adjusted bellows hood *(see Volume 1: Basics and Applications, Chapter 1.4.3 and 2.3)* in order to prevent a reduction of contrast in the photograph. Sinar offers several such aids as part of its building-block system, like wide-angle bellows, standard bellows and multipurpose standard, which can be used effectively and conveniently for focusing observation and as lens hoods.

The Camera –
Which Format?

Basically, the photographer has to decide well in advance of the photographic coverage he is to produce of a building, whether he is going to use a 35 mm or a medium format camera, or whether prefers to employ an adjustable professional camera.

In most cases, the basic question is answered very quickly: the adjustable large format camera is clearly superior to a rigid 35 mm or a rigid medium format camera in two significant respects: First, the large format camera allows the perspective of a photograph to be influenced and vertical and horizontal lines to be corrected or adjusted correctly during the exposure; Second, the large format camera enables the photographer to deliver large format transparencies (from 4 x 5" to 8 x 10") or critically sharp paper prints from large color negatives to his client, with a quality that is decidedly superior to that of any smaller film size, and which also constitute the very best original artwork for

large enlargements. This psychological aspect of the presentation of the finished photographs to the client is an extremely important argument in favor of the large format camera, which should not be underestimated by the photographer.

Rigid Cameras and their
Applications

While the use of 35 mm or medium format cameras for architectural photographs is basically not being rejected, the disadvantages of the photographic technique and of the end product quickly become apparent, the result of the limitations on one hand of a rigid camera construction and on the other of the small film size.

Rigid cameras are suitable for mood pictures and for showing the building in its natural suroundings, when it is not essential to have optimal perspectives, straightened-out verticals and utmost sharpness. For pictures of a more illustrative type, or which have to be taken from unusual camera positions, like pictures taken from a helicopter, the choice very clearly points to the smaller and handier rigid camera design. In spontaneous picture opportunities as well, which should never be underestimated in architectural photography, hand cameras are clearly faster than large format cameras.

The 35 mm camera is also very useful as a "photographic notebook": for the documentation of certain construction stages, or to capture a building at a particular position of the sun, in order to photograph it at a later date with a large format camera and then applying all the refinements of the craft.

It is theoretically possible to use rigid cameras for making photographs of buildings with corrected vertical and horizontal lines. The important requirement in this case is to keep the film plane parallel to the building façade by using a wide angle lens. In practice however, such pictures include far too much surrounding area, which has to be cropped out later, with a corresponding loss of quality resulting from the reduced final format.

Shift lenses are an additional aid that is available for several hand camera systems. But precise settings using their relatively small viewfinders are decidedly more difficult than they are with the large ground glass screen of a large format camera.

Photographs with converging lines can also be corrected with an adjustable enlarger, but with the serious disadvantage that there is no corrected negative, and that the complicated procedure has to be repeated for every subsequent print order

A more recent technique is the subsequent correction of converging lines with electronic image management technology, but here there is a danger of loss of quality

Typical details are often sufficient for the recognition of a familiar building. In this picture, the photographer even omitted the contours of the building, limiting himself to severe cropping. The diagonal composition contributes further tension to the image. Photo by H. G. Esch, Cologne, Germany.

during the conversion of the image information and the reproduction may not be absolutely faithful to the original. All these procedures for the subsequent correction of converging lines are auxiliary, with an inherent sacrifice in quality, and they are also more complicated than an original in-camera correction with an adjustable large format camera.

Adjustable Large Format Cameras and their Applications

Even though large format cameras are less handy and more cumbersome than rigid hand cameras, they will nevertheless always be the preferred instrument for the architectural photographer. The advantages are evident:

● The image format is larger, permitting an optimal presentation to the client. Every client understands that a neatly mounted 8 x 10" transparency "has its price" and that it is more expensive than a contact sheet of 35 mm photographs that have to be viewed with a magnifier. *The advantages of a larger picture format are described in detail in Volume 1: Basics and Applications under Chapter 1.3.*

● The large format of the ground glass screen shows the image in the actual size it will appear in the final transparency or negative, and this makes it much easier for the photographer to judge the composition and to set

the focus with accuracy. Particularly important picture details are recognized more easily – details which on 35 mm and on medium format images are often discovered, much to one's annoyance, only on the finished enlargement. *The advantages of the large ground glass screen image are described in detail in Volume 1: Basics and Applications under Chapter 1.2.*

● The large format camera permits various adjustments, *which are descibed in detail in Volume 1: Basics and Applications under Chapter 4.* We basically differentiate between the axial displacement of the standard in the direction of the optical axis (for focusing and for selecting the image size in close-up photography), the displacements (or shifts) in the four transverse directions (for selecting the exact cropping), and the swings and tilts around the horizontal and/or the vertical axis of the standards (using the rear standard to adjust the perspective and/or the front standard to manipulate the plane of sharpness). Large format cameras are designed according to different principles, and they differ greatly as far as their adjustment capabilities and the ease of operating them are concerned. *Details of this subject can be found in Volume 1: Basics and Applications, Chapters 1.4.2 to 1.4.6.*

● The design of large format cameras, particularly that of the Sinar models, is based on a system concept, so that all components are interchangeable and capable of being assembled to suit specific tasks. The camera can thus be configured exactly for a given picture-taking situation, with special suitability for wide-angle or long lens photography, or for an open choice of formats from 4.5 x 6 cm to 8 x 10".

● The freedom of choice of formats on a large format camera enables the photographer to use the camera with different formats for different tasks. He has a choice of three sheet film formats: 4 x 5", 5 x 7" and 8 x 10" and he can also select one of five rollfilm formats: 4.5 x 6, 6 x 6, 6 x 7, 6 x 9, and 6 x 12 cm. Governed by the range of lenses available for large format cameras, their suitability for wide-angle photography with rollfilm formats is more limited than that of rigid rollfilm cameras. A professional photographer will therefore use this combination (large format camera with rollfilm holder and wide-angle lens) only in exceptional situations, or when he wishes to take advantage of the greater variety of films offered as rollfilms (higher speeds, special films, widely available and processable in more countries).

● The need for an assortment of lenses ranging all the way from an extreme wide-angle lens to an ultra-long focal length lens is especially pronounced in architectural photography. A professional camera must have the special design required to accommodate that range without any compromise whatever. *(See Volume 1: Basics and Applications, Chapter 7.2.)*

Because the precision of the image with corrected verticals is the primary concern in architectural photography, rather than the handiness of the camera, a professional photographer will, in the great majority of cases, opt for the use of a large format camera.

There are basically two camera models available in the Sinar range that are intended for exterior photography: the Sinar f2 and the Sinar p2.

The Sinar f2 was designed as a light camera for exterior photography. Because of its relatively low weight and volume, and also because of the fact that it is fully integrated into the Sinar building-block system, the Sinar f2 is used very often for architectural photography.

The Sinar p2 with its heavy duty construction stands out because of its extraordinary stability. It is used primarily in a studio, however it is equally suitable for exterior photography when its weight and volume are of no consequence. The various models of Sinar cameras are described in detail in *Volume 1: Basics and Applications, Chapter 1.4.6.*

Because extreme wide-angle lenses are used very frequently for architectural photography, the suitability of the camera for such lenses has to be considered *(see Volume 1: Basics and Applications, Chapter 1.4.3)*. On Sinar cameras, this suitability is assured by the flat design of the lens standards and by rail units that can be shortened. There are certain camera designs, however, which become difficult to operate and which have reduced adjustment capability when used with wide-angle lenses.

If one intends to perform architectural photography frequently, one should also tailor one's lens assortment to this application by acquiring wide-angle lenses with the largest possible image circle *(in this regard, see Volume 1: Basics and Applications, Chapter 2)*. Sinaron-W

lenses, which are available with focal lengths from 65 to 155 mm, are particularly desirable, because their large angle of coverage of over 100 degrees permits extreme shifts and tilts.

Special Cameras

Often there are very special instructions by the client that compel the photographer to employ unconventional equipment. A client may ask for a panoramic view of a building that includes the entire surroundings in a 360° view. This situation clearly requires the use of a rotating panorama camera, but usually with a design that permits the lens board to be shifted slightly in the vertical direction, so that verticals can be be corrected.

Another possible request is an overview of a very tight room, which requires the use of a fisheye lens (with a picture angle of up to 180°). These are specialized lenses that are not available for large format cameras, and which can only be found among the accessories offered for 35 mm cameras.

The application of a photogrammetric camera in the field of architecture is another possibility. Especially in the field of building restoration, photogrammetric images are a valuable aid for the architect, because in addition to the perspective views of the building, he can also obtain scaled plans that photogrammetric interpreters can derive from such photographs. This too, requires special photogrammetric cameras that work with 35 mm films or with rollfilms and which are equipped with a grid plate in front of the film plane so that irregularities in film flatness and certain residual lens aberrations can be taken into account during the evaluation.

Another special camera is the endoscopic camera, which can be used for taking extreme close-ups of architectural models simulating the point of view of a person

"La Défense" in Paris, photographed with a rotating panoramic camera. Photo by Alois Stutz, Bremgarten, Switzerland.

inside or outside the future building. Endoscopes are special lenses for 35 mm cameras that are primarily used in medicine, but which are being used more and more for technical applications, such as the architectural views just described.

From the Idea to the Photograph

Every architectural photograph is preceded by a concept, from which a photographer can develop a mental, written or sketched idea for the picture he is to make. More about this subject can be found in the chapter on Photographic Technique, especially in the section on "Visualizing the Photograph". The photographer has to study the object thoroughly long before he ever reaches for his camera. Usually, actual photography is preceded by intensive discussions with the client or with the architect, so that the architect's principal creative ideas can be reflected in the photographs.

Camera Position and Perspective

As already described in detail in *Volume 1: Basics and Applications, Chapters 3, 4.1 and 4.3*, the perspective of a photograph is solely dependent on the camera position. The focal length of the lens affects perspective only in the sense that the object distance required for a wide-angle lens to cover a given subject is shorter than the object distance required for a lens with a long focal length to cover the same subject.

The Focal Length of the Lens as a Styling Tool

During his first walk around the object to be photographed, an experienced photographer will already determine which views (or perspectives) he can record with his equipment and which views are beyond his current scope. This depends on several factors:

● First there is the question whether the vertical lines of a building have to be exactly parallel, or whether a judicious amount of convergence of the vertical lines should beretained in the photograph to emphasize the height and the dynamic of a building in the pictorial expression. *In this regard, see Volume 1: Basics and Applications, Practical Examples 1 and 3.*

● The use of an extreme wide-angle lens requires an equally extreme wide-angle suitability of the camera. *See Volume 1: Basics and Applications, Chapters 1.4.2 and 1.4.3.* If a residual convergence of the verticals can be tolerated or if it is perhaps even desired by the client, then the perspective introduced in a photograph by means of an appropriate wide-angle lens can be more extreme than it would have to be if the verticals were to be completely parallel. It is good practice to submit both versions to the client: A partially corrected extreme wide-angle view with gently converging verticals, and a second view with completely corrected verticals and a

The long focal length that was required produced a strong compression of the object space. Photo: Chris Cascoigne, London.

An extremely short focal length imbues the picture with a very strong spatial effect. Photo: Hardev Singh, New Delhi, India.

mild perspective. Experience shows that the client will usually accept both versions and use them for different purposes.

● Often there are local obstacles as well that force the photographer to make compromises. For instance, there may not be enough unobstructed space in front of the building for him to make the extreme wide-angle photograph he had planned to make. In such cases it is often advisable to assess the situation again from a greater distance. Perhaps the possibility exists of making the photograph from a nearby building, which would result in a slightly milder, but seldom seen perspective, coming from an entirely new angle and creating a pictorial expression that makes the building look quite different. Cars in parking places can also mean time-consuming problems for the photographer, often spoiling an otherwise perfect plan. There may also be stationary obstacles, like power lines, signs, street lamps, or obstructing trees, all of which can cause problems and limitations for the photographer.

Even though perspective is only indirectly dependent on the focal length of a lens, the lens and with it the choice of the angle of view, is one of the most important creative aids in architectural photography.

Shifts of the Image and Lens Standards as Styling Means

It should be stated right at the beginning: architectural photographs that show only corrected vertical lines are boring in the long run. The dynamic, particular in the case of tall buildings, only becomes truly effective when these lines, by their very convergence emphasize the impressive height of the building. Hardly any photographer would have the idea of showing the World Trade Center, the Empire State Building, or other awesome concrete giants with straightened-out vertical lines. The pedestrian in the street too, turns his gaze sharply upwards to view these skyscrapers. He hardly notices the strongly converging vertical lines only because our sense of equilibrium processes the verticals with our stereoscopic visual and mental capabilities: our brain knows that these lines are really parallel, and it simulates that parallelism to us while we are looking at them. Even buildings that have no vertical lines, like the Cheops Pyramid, require a veretical setting of the image standard, because the Pyramid would otherwise be reproduced with a compression of the height.

Matters are different with horizontal lines. Extremely converging horizontal lines, like the uncorrected horizontal lines we see on a long row of house fronts, are much less disturbing to us. *Practical Example 4 in Volume 1: Basics*

Only in rare instances are very tall buildings depicted without converging lines. Appropriate shifts of the front and/or back standards position the building's predominant lines in space in a way that creates a dynamic pictorial effect.
Photo by Waltraud Krase, Frankfurt, Germany.

and Applications illustrates this impression. In this case we are free, within a relatively large latitude, to correct the converging horizontal lines, to leave them unchanged, or to emphasize them. This enables us to create viewing effects that are still perceived as natural, even though they deviate strongly from the original perspective.

An experienced architectural photographer will devote much more thought to the perspective of horizontal lines than he will to verticals. Here too, the movements available on a large format camera that permit a parallel horizontal shift constitute an ideal tool for cultivating a personal style and for achieving perfect architectural photographs.

There cannot be a general statement, of course, as to whether a photograph should be corrected in the vertical and/or in the horizontal direction. This would depend on the building and on the situation on one hand, but also, on the technical characteristics of the camera. With a rigid camera, even when used with a shift lens, (sometimes wrongly called a perspective control lens) the limitations are clearly established. But among professional cameras as well, significant differences in design become quickly apparent during extreme displacements, and this in turn affects the extent of the evolution and cultivation of a photographer's personal style. As a rule, one should always select a camera system that allows the greatest possible technical latitude for pictorial creativity when a photograph is being made.

Swings and Tilts of the Image and Lens Standards as Styling Means

Swings and tilts, which are explained in detail in *Volume 1: Basics and Applications, Chapter 4.3.2,* very often are not significant in architectural photography be-

Vignetting problems can be eliminated with modest swings. The plane of sharpness can also be positioned in space in such a way that the entire façade will be perfectly sharp at full aperture. In this picture, the photographer incorporated a tree as an additional creative element.
Photo by H. G. Esch, Cologne, Germany.

cause of the small scale of reproduction. Depth of field is usually more than sufficient for rendering the building and its surroundings in focus from the near foreground to infinity.

Certain situations can arise, however, when a sharpness compensation may still become necessary. For instance when there is an extremely close foreground and when the building is so extensive that it exceeds the normal depth of field. The photographer may also be asked to photograph an architectural model to a scale such that a sharpness compensation becomes necessary, in order for that model to appear sharp from front to rear.

Another instance occurs when extreme views of façades are requested, which may require such an extreme shift of the standard in order to straighten the verticals,

that the limit of vignetting of the lens would be exceeded. In order to prevent a darkening of the corners of the image, the lens can be tilted at the same time that a sharpness compensation is being made, thus eliminating the vignetting problem.

When details of a façade are to be photographed, selective sharpness can be used as a creative tool, in order to make that particular façade stand out from a multitude of adjacent houses. The large format camera is especially well suited for such tasks. The larger the film format (the largest being 8 x 10"), the longer the focal length of the lens and the larger the working aperture that is chosen, the more selectively can the range of sharpness be controlled by tilting the standards.

Photographic Technique

Photographic technique for architectural photography is not just limited to the correct operation of the camera or to the straightening out of vertical and horizontal lines. Those are merely the prerequisites for the production of acceptable photographs of architectural objects that distinguish themselves qualitatively from amateur photographs (which every architect or construction boss can make himself).

Prerequisites for Photography

Even experienced photographers first devote intensive mental attention to a building before touching a camera. The creative intentions of the architect must also be taken into consideration, as well as the feasibility of incorporating them in his photographs. Which elements of his building does the architect want especially emphasized; which of these elements are needed for the building to make the same impression on the viewer in a photograph as it would in reality? Which light conditions will show off the best side of the building to its greatest advantage? Would it be flat lighting to bring out colors and spatial design dramatically, or should the façade be shown in grazing light, so that its structure is shown more effectively? Which of the surrounding elements that might affect the building in a positive or negative manner have to be taken into account? Which of these elements should or even must be included in the photograph, and which should be hidden or shown in such a way that the viewer will no longer notice unsightly details? These are but a few of the many questions with which the photographer has to concern himself during the preparatory phase of his assignment.

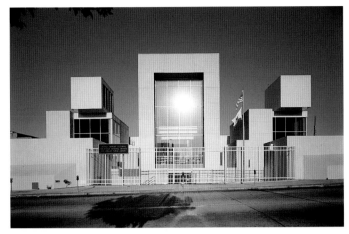

In order to work fast and safely, all camera positions should be determined before actual photography takes place.

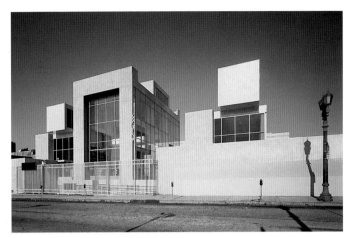

A change of camera position of only a few feet can result in an entirely different perspective. Photos: Waltraud Krase, Frankfurt

How to Plan Architectural Photographs

The preliminary discussion with the architect or the client is one step, the inspection of the location is the second step. Both are indispensable for the photographer to achieve an optimal performance by producing photographs that show the building in the manner envisioned by the architect or the client.

Visualizing the Photograph

During the first inspection of the site to be photographed, the Sinar adjustable format mask is exceedingly useful. It helps the photographer to select a camera position for the best perspective during his first reconnoitering walk

The impression of this building is accentuated by its partially straightened vertical lines. Photo: H.G. Esch, Cologne, Germany.

around the area, which determines the focal length of the lens to be used. By holding the mask in the appropriate manner in front of our viewing eye, it can already simulate the camera adjustments that will be needed, and it will also make it evident right away whether certain adjustments are at all feasible. *Practical Example 2 in Volume 1: Basics and Applications* explains its use.

Armed with a format mask and a note pad, the photographer walks around the many-sided subject that he plans to photograph. In this instance, many-sided is meant quite literally, because the architects' ideas often present themselves at least as impressively on the rear or side façades as they do on the much-photographed front of the building. During the inspection walk, it is always advisable first to view the building from a greater distance. Only when one has a clear sense of what parts of the surroundings should be included in the pictures and which parts should be toned down or even suppressed, should one walk around the building in closer circles to look for important details and extreme perspectives.

Here is where the notebook is important, for general comments and also for tentative thoughts about which photographs could be made at what position of he sun. It might be quite useful to document the most important views with a 35 mm or an instant camera, especially when the photographer, unable to execute the final work himself, has to delegate it to a colleague or to an assistant. In this case, a sketch of the grounds with distances and directions becomes a valuable communication aid that greatly facilitates the preparations for the job.

Experienced architectural photographers who work effectively and successfully with large format cameras, use this method to determine every camera position and the required focal length in advance. It is remarkable how quickly the various photographs of the assignment can then be completed. This procedure, makes a supremely professional impression on the client, who often wishes to be present when the photographs are being made.

Often it is worthwhile to repeat a particular photograph at different times of the day.

That gives the client the opportunity to select the most suitable image. Photos by Hardev Singh, New Delhi, India.

Geographical and Meteorological Problems

Compared to many other subjects that photographers have to deal with, architectural structures are stubborn and unyielding. They cannot be turned around or shifted, and they do not care about what the photographer has in mind with them.

The photographer has to suit himself to them, he often has to be content with unsightly or unfinished surroundings, and he has to disguise unattractive parts in such a way that the viewer will no longer notice them in the final photograph. That is architectural photography.

But it is not only the neighboring building that gives us grief, because they block the space needed for an overall view or because they cast a shadow on the building just when the light is ideal for photography: there are countless troublesome details on the building itself. Venetian blinds, open windows, laundry hung to dry outside a window somewhere on the 13th floor – just before the photograph was to be taken, of course – these are unnerving details that confirm to every experienced architectural photographer that the cooperation of an assistant and the use of two-way radio communication are absolutely hot tips.

In addition to the good spirits therare also the bad ones. The weather, for instance: everything is perfect for the photograph to be taken, five minutes ago, the assistant persuaded a truck driver to hold off unloading an urgent shipment in front of the building – but a ridiculous ugly little cloud just won't move out of the way of the sun... That too, is architectural photography.

Or what tales of woe can the out-of-town photographer tell, who has been waiting for three days for the weather to clear, even though the forecast had been favorable...?

The weather forecast too, is part of the planning process for the photograph. It is advisable for the architectural photographer to become somewhat familiar with meteorology, at least to the extent that he can understand flight weather forecasts that can be obtained at regional weather stations or at airports. That avoids many costly waiting periods, which the client will find plausible only after much persuasion.

The Structure in Favorable Light

The light too, holds not a few surprises for the photographer, it is another parameter to which he has to adapt himself completely. It is not only that ugly little cloud that always blocks the sun just at the decisive moment, but the direction of the light in general, which is quite likely not to be favorable on the preferred shooting date that was reserved on the calendar.

Already during the first reconnoitering visit it is important to check the path of the sun and to think about the best times of the day for photography. In time, one gains experience with such matters and one senses, even during the first walk around the project, approximately at what time of the day the sun will be in the ideal position. However one can often be mistaken, especially if one has to make photographs in an entirely different meridional region. The path of the sun is quite different in Stockholm for instance, than it is in Rome or in Cairo, and the 40°-light that is good in northern latitudes, is tinged with the red cast of dawn or sunset in equatorial countries. Here too, a thorough reconnaissance is the guarantee for better photographs. To be safe, especially in foreign countries, a photographer should plan more than one day for an important building.

If there are several objects to be photographed within an accessible distance, and if the time available for the project is limited, it is worthwhile to travel to different buildings at different times of day. In addition to the bad spirits that want to spoil the photographs, there are also good spirits that now and then surprise the photographer with a lucky chance that is unique and that leads to a super photograph that could hardly have been planned any better.

Another tip from experience: more even than in the photography of objects or landscapes, a polarizing filter *(see Volume 1: Basics and Applications, Chapter 6.1.7.)* is an enormously important accessory for reducing reflections on façades and for making the blue sky appear darker. Conversion filters too *(see Volume 1: Basics and Applications, Chapter 6.1.3)*, are occasionally useful in color photography for the correction of color casts that are inherent in the light of dawn or sunset.

Natural and Artificial Light Sources as Creative Tools

Light is the most important creative tool in photography altogether. More than seventy years ago, Léonard Misonne already realized that "The subject is nothing, the light is everything". Those who are familiar with his exquisite landscape paintings know what Misonne meant by that, and his statement is just as applicable to architectural photography: the greater the atmosphere created by the light, the more unique, interesting and original is the impression created by an architectural photograph. It is worthwhile for the photographer to visit the structure at all times of the day, especially during morning or evening times, in order to take advantage of special lighting moods to capture unusual and therefore more impressive photographs.

In twilight especially, the photographer can encounter the best opportunities for superb photographs. But this very endeavor requires some staging: which windows should be lit, where would darkness be more appropriate to make a façade of windows look more natural? In such cases, one often has to rely on the understanding and the cooperation of the inhabitants or the building supervisor, and once again portable radio communication proves to be a precious secret tip. At twilight, however, speed is of the essence, because optimal lighting lasts only a few minutes before the dramatic light of sundown fades away or before the warm light of dawn turns into pale daylight.

Architectural photographs taken at night also have a very special charm. Here too, controlling the lights in the rooms is as essential as it is for twilight photography, and frequently there is the problem of light reflections on the glass façades, which are quite irrelevant during the day and which therefore cannot be judged properly during the reconnoitering trip.

The question of appropriate artificial lighting is, of course, particularly relevant for interior architectural photographs. It is basically important that every light should only be used for fill-in illumination, so that it will not alter the natural play of light planned by the architect, and thus preserve its effect on the architecture. Fill-in light should never stand out. It should merely ensure that shaded areas become discernible and that good shadow detail is achieved.

That presents the photographer with light measurement problems. Lighting and exposure have to be correlated in such a way that both the views through the windows and the shaded portions inside the rooms are reproduced with good detail. The Sinar expolux System

  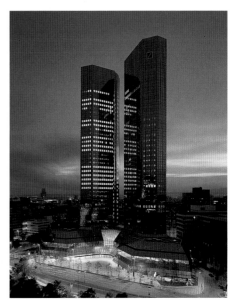

Photographs at dusk demand the highest concentration on the part of the photographer, because the lighting changes completely in the space of only a few minutes. Photo by Reinhart Wolf, Hamburg, Germany.

is the ideal tool in this situation. A detailed explanation of its practical application and the lighting of such back-lit situations is covered by *Chapter 5 of Volume 1: Basics and Applications*. More compact and easier to transport, but less versatile than the expolux System is the Sinar Booster used in conjunction with the portable Minolta Exposure Meter III or IV.

Interior and Exterior Architecture

A single photograph is hardly ever sufficient to portray the character of a building to its very best advantage. As a rule, a series of pictures is necessary for the ideas of the architect and for the diversity of his work to be properly expressed and documented photographically.

The surroundings of the building, to which the architect usually gives serious consideration while developing his concept, are an important factor in architectural photographs. It is an entirely different task whether the architect is to design a single-family dwelling that will be located in the open countryside and which should not disturb that countryside, or whether he is to design an office complex that must on one hand project a certain company image

Mixed light situations create special problems with respect to color reproduction. Photo by Peter Seidel, Frankfurt, Germany.

while on the other hand it must blend into a neighborhood of other office and industrial buildings.

In order for the photographer to express the architect's idea as favorably as possible, a number of interior photographs are needed in addition to the series of exterior photographs. For example, how does the entrance are present itself to a visitor? Which details did he architect design in a particularly original manner, further enhancing the style of the building? What light brings out important structures in the interior spaces, and what time of day is best for good photographs of such interesting details? What are the office areas like? Do they appear sober and functional, thus not requiring special photographic documentation, or did the architect incorporate certain creative elements that should be photographed particularly effectively? Can the interior photographs be made with existing light or will artificial light sources be needed, which may even have to be combined with the available light in complicated mixed-light photographs?

All of the above are questions that confront the architectural photographer while he is planning and photographing a building, and which in the long run make his job versatile and interesting

Film Materials

An architectural photographer has basically four different film materials at his disposal: color transparency films, color negative films, black-and-white films, and instant photography materials.

Photographing on Sheet Films

Color transparencies continue to be the most frequently used film material, because the printing industry has given preference to this type of original for decades, all the more so with the growing use of scanners. It is also the accepted procedure for the photographer to deliver a transparency to his client, thus freeing himself from filing responsibilities and from requests for duplicates. The downside of this procedure is the fact that the photographer loses control over the use of his photographs. It is usually possible also to have color enlargements made from transparencies, either on reversal paper or via an internegative. The established procedure, however, is to use original color negatives for the production of color enlargements.

Color negatives are often made only as a companion shot for a color transparency, in case the client later requests color enlargements, possibly as construction

Whenever possible, the surrounding setting of a building should be incorporated in a photograph. Photo by Peter Seidel, Franfurt, Germany.

Differences in color temperature are especially effective in views of interiors with artificial light hat also have windows to the outside. Photo by H. G. Esch, Cologne, Germany.

records or for presentation purposes. More and more color enlargements are now being used as original art for the printer, in part because it is easy to have a new paper enlargement made, so that the danger of damage at the lithographer's is of less consequence than it is for an original, unique transparency. The color negative, i.e. the production of a paper print has the added advantage that density and colors can be further corrected. Aside from these considerations, it is also possible to have large format color transparencies made from original color negatives, using special print films.

Black-and-white films are still being used quite frequently for architectural photography. First of all, architecture lends itself exceedingly well to black-and-white photography; second, with black-and-white films one has the added option of using filters to achieve tonal separation between buildings and sky, and to accentuate cloud formations, and third, black-and-white prints are frequently used as original art for printing brochures and technical articles. Aside from that, a great many pictures for construction status documentation are made only in black-and-white, primarily because of cost considerations.

Instant photography is used comparatively seldom for architectural photography, certainly much less than in studio photography. Understandably, instant prints, which are available both in color and in black-and-white in the sizes 8 x 10 cm and 4 x 5", are used when the client needs a picture immediately. Very often the same photograph is made on conventional films as well, and later delivered as the final picture with the option of having enlargements produced to any desired size.

Many phoytographers use costly instant photographs only for control purposes, to check contrast and exposure. In a way, the expensive high-quality instant are too good

for this purpose, because most photographers do not retain these control prints, throwing them away instead. This method should not really be necessary anyway, if the exposure measurement technique is mastered correctly.

What type of film should be used? An architectural photographer is best served if he routinely makes every photograph on color transparency film and on color negative film as well, perhaps even on black-and-white film in addition. He then has the ideal base in the original quality for any subsequent need and he would not be dependent on internegatives, which always entail a loss of quality as compared to an original photograph. The use of three different types of films has an additional advantage: something may go wrong in the laboratory, but it is highly unlikely that it would occur simultaneously during the processing of the color transparency film and the color negative film as well. If one of his photographs is damaged, the photographer would always have the same photograph on the other type of film, from which he could still produce any desired end product by using an internegative or print film. If, on the other hand, the photographer used only one type of film and if there is a processing malfunction or a loss in the mails, his only recourse is to repeat the photographs – without being reimbursed by anyone for all that extra work...

Mishaps in processing are not the only hazard that the photographer may have to deal with. Films can get lost in the mails, or the cartons with the precious light-sensitive content can get damaged en route. That is why experienced photographers do not ship color transparencies and color negatives to their professional lab in a single package, but in two separate packages, often even at different times. Over the years, these precautions prove to be worthwhile.

Outdoor photography with sheet films has the disadvantage that it may occasionally be necessary to reload film holders in total darkness. Sinar offers a very practical accessory for this purpose: the *Black Box*. A light-tight film changing bag is built into this "portable darkroom", with which exposed films can be removed from the film holders and new ones loaded without any difficulty in a car or in the hotel, and in broad daylight. Contained in an elegant attaché case, the Black Box also has interior compartments for film holders and sheet films.

An alternative to traditional sheet films are the Ready-Load or Quick-Load Films available from Fuji, Kodak and Polaroid. These are color transparency films for the E-6 Process, packaged in light-tight paper sleeves that can be exposed in 4 x 5" instant film cassettes. This eliminates having to load sheet film holders in the dark. As practical as these convenient pre-loaded films are when a photographer is on the road, there are two disadvantages to be considered: one, film flatness in the cassette is not sufficient for precision work, because the sheet film hangs freely in the cassette, supported only on two sides. Film flatness is considerably worse than it is in traditional 4 x 5" film holders, and it cannot be compared with the film flatness in a Sinar sheet film holder, which features a full-surface pressure plate and an extremely precise film seating. The second disadvantage comes from the perforations for tearing the films off, which may lead to scratches during processing.

Unfortunately the range of sheet films in the 4 x 5", 5 x 7" and 8 x 10" sizes is somewhat sparse and limited to a speed of ISO 100/21° and ISO 200/24°. Films with the ISO 400/27° speed, which meanwhile have demonstrated outstanding quality in the 35 mm format, would save the day for the photographer in many critical situations.

Photographing on Roll Film

In many instances, making the photographs on roll film is an alternative to the use of sheet films that is very much worth considering, especially because Sinar offers an outstanding roll film holder, with a freely adjustable picture format from 4.6 x 6 to 6 x 12 cm. Both types of film have their advantages and disadvantages.

When the smaller of the rollfilm formats are used on a Sinar camera with its professional lenses, the choice of extreme wide-angle lenses is very limited when compared with the selection available, for instance, for the corresponding medium medium-format cameras. The lens with the shortest focal length that can be used on a 4 x 5" large format camera is a 65 mm lens, which is not an impressive wide-angle lens, for example, for a 6 x 7 cm format. That naturally places a considerable constraint on creative freedoms in architectural photography.

The great advantage of the use of roll films is that films do not have to be loaded in total darkness, which is so often a problem in outdoor photography and which is also time-consuming. Furthermore, roll films are not only more readily available than sheet films in all countries around the world, but they are also available in a significantly greater variety, including the high speed films sought after by many photographers for those critical sitiuations where the conventional ISO 100/21° films barely fill the neeed, and then only with much manipulation.

The fact that the use of roll films results in smaller transparencies and negatives appears to be a disadvantage. But one must not pre-judge the good quality of roll films without actually testing them. The majority of photographs taken by architectural photographers are used in a final format smaller than 5 x 7", and then only for printed reproduction. Even if the client should occasionally request an 8 x 10" or 11 x 14" enlargement, the quality of a $2^1/_4$ x $3^1/_2$" negative is still satisfactory, resulting in no discernible loss of sharpness or increase in graininess.

The Subject of Formats from Another Point of View

The format used when taking a photograph, whether it is on roll film in the 6 x 7 cm size (which, incidentally, has the same proportions as 4 x 5" and 8 x 10"!) or whether it is on 4 x 5", 5 x 7" or even 8 x 10" sheet film should be of no concern to the client. What matters to the client is first, the size of the photographs that are delivered, and second, the basic question whether the quality of the photographs is appropriate for their intended application.

The advantage of the large format is that a transparency or a negative, even the smallest of the large formats of 4 x 5", has sufficient quality for most every need, even if the client who ordered a picture for a publicity folder later decides to order a giant enlargement for a trade show stand.

The 4 x 5" size is probably the most often used size in architectural photography. On one hand, the quality of this size is satisfactory for more than 90 percent of the final applications, and on the other hand, a 4 x 5" camera is much handier and lighter for outdoor photography than an 8 x 10" camera, for instance. Nevertheless one should not neglect the psychological aspect at the time the photographs are presented to the client: an 8 x 10" transparency, neatly framed in the proper cardboard mount, can be sold more readily and at a higher price than a mere 4 x 5" image that is only one fourth as big as the 8 x 10" transparency. That is a fact that always favors the larger picture size.

Urs Tillmanns

Check List for Architectural Photographs

What are the client's requirements?

_____

_____

_____

_____

1. Can the task be accomplished?

1.1 ❑ yes → skip to item 2
1.2 ❑ no → wait, notify client
      explain reasons:
      ❑ Temporary reasons, such as:
        – Building / Surroundings not ready → wait
        – Weather / Lighting unsuitable (→ see items 7 / 8)
      ❑ Technical reasons, such as:
        – Geometrical and optical limitations of the camera
        – Local limitations of the surrounding situation
      → Suggest alternatives to the client

2 Do vertical or horizontal building lines have to be straightened?

2.1 ❑ yes → skip to item 3.2
2.2 ❑ no → continue at item 3.1

3 What type of camera is to be used?

3.1 ❑ Rigid camera, 35 mm or medium format, with corresponding lenses and accessories; → continued under item 6
3.2 ❑ Adjustable large format camera; → continued under item 4

4 What film format is desired?

4.1 ❑ < 4 x 5" → large format camera with rollfilm holder and 65, 75 and 90 mm lenses; → see item 6
4.2 ❑ ≥ 4 x 5" → continued under item 5

5 Which lenses are needed?

Format	4 x 5"	5 x 7"	8 x 10"
Extreme wide-angle	65, 75 mm	90 mm	120 mm
Wide-angle	90 mm	135 mm	180 mm
Normal focal length	150 mm	220 mm	300 mm
Long focal length	240 mm	360 mm	480 mm

6 What type of film will be required?

6.1 ❑ Color transparency film
6.2 ❑ Color negative film
6.3 ❑ Black-and-white film
6.4 ❑ Instant material (only 8 x 10 cm and 4 x 5")

7 What time of day is best for the photograph?

7.1 ❑ Dawn, → see 11.1
7.2 ❑ 8 am to 10 am, → see 11.1
7.3 ❑ 10 am to 12 noon
7.4 ❑ 12 noon to 2 pm
7.5 ❑ 2 pm to 4 pm
7.6 ❑ 4 pm to 7 pm, → see 11.1
7.7 ❑ Evening twilight, → see 11.1
7.8 ❑ Night-time photograph at _____ → see 11.1

8 What light conditions are ideal?

8.1 ❑ Sun with a clear sky
8.2 ❑ Sun with interesting cloud formations
8.3 ❑ Diffused light
8.4 ❑ Cloudy

9 Is artificial light needed for fill-in purposes?

9.1 ❑ Exterior photographs only, → move on to 11
9.2 ❑ Interior photographs as well, → move on to 10

10 Is artificial light needed for fill-in purposes?

10.1 ❑ No, interior rooms do not have high contrast
10.2 ❑ No, interior rooms do not have high contrast
10.3 ❑ Lighting of inside rooms in daylight
10.4 ❑ Photography at night with complete lighting of rooms

11 Will filters be needed?

11.1 ❑ Conversion filters, color correction filters
11.2 ❑ Polarizing filters (glass façades, cloud enhancement)
11.3 ❑ Contrast filters for black-and-white photographs

12 What special preparations will have to be made for these photographs?

12.1 ❑ Assistant needed (colleague, apprentice)
12.2 ❑ Notify custodian / owner / tenant / police
12.3 ❑ Changes in the surrounding situation
12.4 ❑ Are there special obstacles that must be taken into account?
12.5 ❑ Are certain objects in the vicinity to be included in the photograph?
12.6 ❑ Can film holders be loaded?
        ❑ Yes   ❑ No
12.7 ❑ Required means of transportation:
        ❑ Car
        ❑ Rental car
        ❑ Public transportation
        ❑ Airplane

Attach a sketch of the location and a description of the subject!

Hans Georg Esch

"The fascination of space and light motivated me to take up architectural photography. To me the latter means a constant deliberation of 'constructed' space, perspective and light."

A freelance photographer since 1988, Hans Georg Esch has been operating his own studio in Cologne, Germany since 1990. Architectural photography became one of his favorite subjects early during his training, and the many awards that his pictures received at competitions and workshops attest to his special skills in dealing with the forms and spaces of architecture.

Hans Georg Esch does not merely capture the fascination of space, planes and lines in his architectural photographs, he adds his own personal creative touches that lend a captivating new expression to architecture. This photographer brings new creative elements to bear in his pictures, giving the viewer a fresh look at familiar, often photographed architecture.

Contrast is one of Esch's favorite creative elements. With consummate skill, he combines light and shade, curves and edges into an entirely new creative image, and he positions his buildings in the picture area with such accomplished formal cropping that the viewer perceives it as a perfect composition. Nothing needs to be changed or improved. With the aid of architecture, the photographer has created a new, independent work of art.

"Can a photograph be a work of art? Is photography an art?" asks art historian Ralf Leisner while looking at Esch's pictures. "If photography is currently playing a central role in the art scene, it is because of its challenge to the spectrum of the classical concept of art and because of its subjective documentation of artifacts that stimulates new modes of perception in the viewer. Esch's exploration of architecture meets these conditions by means of judicious renewal of the visible. From formal, monochromatic stylizing to complex experimentation with postmodern architecture, Esch magically choreographs a building into a work of art."

Hans Georg Esch creates an extremely interesting and well-balanced image composition that preserves the spaciousness that the buildings in his architectural photographs need for their particular lines and space-determining planes to achieve their intended impact. He also knows how to utilize this spaciousness for optimum pictorial effect, for instance by incorporating the vapor trail of an aircraft in the composition so skillfully that it appears to belong there. Or he juxtaposes the gentle lines of the Düsseldorf Playhouse with the sharp contours of a building opposite, thus creating a contrast that enhances the impression that the architect strove to create with his building.

Robert Polidori

"To me, architectural photography is more than just documentation. I want my pictures to make the viewer experience the aura of a bygone era and sense the secrets that these legendary walls contain."

Canadian-born Robert Polidori grew up in the United States of America, where he studied the History of Art at the State University of New York at Buffalo, NY. He then worked for nearly three years as an assistant to film maker Jona Mekas, only to become more and more interested in still photography.

In 1983 Polidori embarked on the costly and time-consuming project of photographing the Palace of Versailles during its restoration. He makes the following comments about his pictures:

"Is there anyone who never sensed a special atmosphere, an undefinable odor when he or she first entered an unfamiliar room? Do these sensations not conjure an impression of all the events, of all the silences and all the emotions that this room once witnessed? Why should these walls not have absorbed all the impressions and all the experiences of their inhabitants and guests like a film and hidden them within themselves?

Like a metaphor, like a catalyst of our *spiritual condition*, the room always strikes us as the revelation of a psychic and spiritual universe. An old proverb admonishes us, not without foundation: *Walls have ears*. They also have the appearance and the aura of a bygone era.

The recent restoration of the central building of the *Palais de Versailles* to its condition at the time of Louis XV represents the crowning achievement of an entire series of restoration projects that began after the end of World War II.

The first glimpse strikes us as inappropriate, because it imparts the viewer with a profound impression of visual illusions. Upon closer scrutiny of this apparent peculiarity, and of these strange surroundings, the dissonance diminishes and points, regardless of the prevailing untidiness, to the logic of the future.

We will never be able to rid ourselves of the notion that the invisible purpose of this impression means nothing more than the visualization of the subconscious wish to prove that the past can come alive again and that the spirit can be reincarnated."

Polidori's photographs of Versailles are contained in a 420-page book published simultaneously in 1991 by the three publishing houses Editions Mendès in France, Abbeville Press in the United States and Magnus in Italy.

Robert Polidori's pictures speak their own language within architectural photography. Not only is Polidori an accomplished master of formal composition and of large format technique, he also achieves an extraordinarily high contrast in his images while maintaining remarkable shadow detail. The secret is in the refined light measurement on one hand, and on the other, in his use of color negative film for artificial light with a conversion filter in daylight. With this technique, Polidori depicts the historical rooms of Vesailles bathed in such a rich atmosphere of mixed light that they look as if time in them had stood still.

Reinhart Wolf

"I love heights, and I feel that the tops of New York's skyscrapers express the strength and the spirit of America."

"I love heights," said Reinhart Wolf during an interview with American art guru Andy Warhol, "and I have the feeling that the tops of New York's skyscrapers express the strength and the spirit of America. New York inspires me – its skyscrapers are like phallic symbols of fertility.

I wanted to photograph the buildings while they were still there. There is construction going on everywhere. Many of the buildings that I wanted to photograph have already been torn down."

Reinhart Wolf, born in Berlin in 1930, son of an architect, was fascinated by New York City. In particular the variety of architectural styles is astounding, as is the fact that hardly anybody is aware of the interesting details on the tops of the giant buildings. However the idea of photographing this unique world of architecture by itself did not come from Reinhart Wolf, but from his friend Thomas Höpker, who was then the chief editor of the German magazine 'Geo'. "Reinhart, just look at those fascinating pinnacles!" said Höpker to Wolf as they were looking at the New York skyline from the 33rd floor of one of the buildings. "Incredible – yet hardly anybody has ever seen these beautiful architectural details. Why don't you photograph them for us?"

Wolf made his task anything but easy. He selected an 8 x 10" Sinar camera for making these photographs from the highest rooftops in New York, using lenses with such extremely long focal lengths as 360, 480, 600 all the way to 1000 mm to fill the frame with the exquisite details of the tops of skyscrapers across the way. He supported an extra-long Sinar rail equipped with several multipurpose standards and bellows units on two tripods, which he anchored down even further in particularly precarious situations.

Aside from these technical problems there was the additional need to obtain prior permission for access to the top floors. Not just during office hours, but five o'clock in the morning, for instance, because that is when the rising sun bathed the concrete giants in a truly fantastic light...

Wolf could have made his job a lot easier by using a 4 x 5" camera. The images might have been slightly less sharp and they might not enlarge quite as well, but even so they would have become a sensation. What motivated Wolf to select the largest of the formats was the large focusing screen and the ability to check every detail on it for maximum sharpness. This provided Wolf with the assurance that his photographs – the result of painstaking preparations and perseverance – will have been made with the very best possible quality.

Everything had to be just right for Wolf: the light, clouds, lighted windows, reflections on the glass façades. And he demanded the same precision of the ground glass image – and of the camera.

Hardev Singh

"In my architectural photographs, especially those for my hotel clients, the ambiance in the picture is the most important factor. The gentle mood of dusk and tastefully lighted interiors beckon the guest into an atmosphere designed to make him feel relaxed."

More than 15 years ago, when Hardev Singh first took up professional photography, there was no professional training available in India. Professional photography was not yet widespread in India at that time. Only a few who could afford a camera and who were able to obtain film material from overseas on a regular basis, were practicing that profession.

Hardev Singh did everything himself. He is self-taught in photography, and he was one of the first persons in India to work with an adjustable large format camera. Singh attended courses and workshops in other countries, and he assembled his own color laboratory, because the few color labs that existed in India at the time simply did not have the equipment or the know-how required for the standard of quality that Singh wanted to offer his clients. The number of his customers gradually increased. Industrial firms needed pictures of their installations and products for their advertising literature, architects needed pictorial documentation of their projects, and the hotels that were springing up everywhere urgently needed color transparencies so that travel agencies in the rich western countries could publicize them.

That is how Hardev Singh came to specialize in hotel photography, and his name quickly became familiar to the managers of the Sheratons, Hyatts and Kempinskis. To date he has photographed more than 150 hotels in 36 countries.

"Every hotel is different," explains Singh. "Each one has its own charm, its own character and peculiarity that have to be communicated by the photographs. In order to recognize the important details that matter, one has to be very familiar with the hotel business. One has to know how the hotel works, how it is organized. The ambiance is important, and the photographs have to convey it as it really is. That is why all my photographs are characteristically made with available light, and flash is used only very sparsely for fill-in illumination. Technical support too, is most important in hotel photography. I always travel with three assistants with whom I have been working for many years. We are a well-coordinated team and each one knows exactly what must be done. Speed and safety are required as well, because it is not acceptable for us to interfere with their normal business for very long and it simply must not happen that we have to repeat a photograph just because we had not noticed a few creases in a table cloth ..."

Approximately half of Hardev Singh's gross income is generated by hotel photography. The rest comes from architectural and industrial photography within India itself. "And there will be many assignments in this field in the coming years," smiles Singh, "because we are in the middle of an economic upsurge."

Chris Gascoigne

"Good architectural photography consists as much of what is omitted or suggested as that which is actually depicted. I prefer to compose my photographs from the center outwards."

Chris Gascoigne has been active as an independent photographer for only four years. Before that he had temporary jobs, and after his studies at the London College of Printing, he completed his training with the highest awards.

"For a long time, especially during my college years, Henri Cartier-Bresson and Josef Koudelka were my role models" remembers Chris Cascoigne, "and I tried to emulate their distinctive styles. Then, all of a sudden, their way of taking pictures struck me as somehow superseded, almost archaic, perfect for art galleries, but not suitable in this day and age for illustrating articles in magazines and other periodicals. The world has changed, and photography too, has become more commercial and more short-lived".

"It was also during my last college years that I had my first practical experiences with a Sinar camera", continues Chris Gascoigne, "which, with its adjustment capabilities and the way perspectives can be corrected in architectural and interior photographs, matched my concept of photography exactly. Large format photography had drawn me into its spell, and after six months, which I used full-time for the production of a presentable portfolio, my photographic career began for real".

Chris Gascoigne leaves nothing to chance in his architectural photography. That a passing suburban train can be seen through a passageway of a building is just as deliberate as the two persons that can be seen behind the glass walls of an entrance way. They add life to the picture and they show the architecture in an environment of natural goings-on. And composition too, the arrangement of architectural elements within the frame, stems from a special flair for forms and for interior design. In Chris Gascoigne's opinion, composition and precise color reproduction are the most important elements of photography. He uses a Sinar p2 camera with ten Sinaron lenses and approximately 50 Sinar Color Control Filters. Depending on the light conditions, he chooses certain Fuji or Kodak Ektachrome Films, and he masters even the most complicated mixed light situations with great care and experience, plus some tricks, like fill-in flash with filters. He selects the exact framing right on the ground glass screen. "That is really a great plus for large format photography", he explains. "The large image on the ground glass screen is indispensable for meticulous composition. I detest those wideangle shots that simply include everything and which one later keeps chopping down until a reasonably acceptable framing is reached. I much prefer to use for a long focal length lens, say 115 or even 300 mm, and I try to use interesting details to compose the image from he center outward. Most of my assignments place the greatest demands on me, but then large format photography is exceedingly satisfying. I hope I may cultivate this kind of work for another 30 years".

Gabriele Basilico

"Landscape is an important element in architectural photography. It enhances pictorial expression and places buildings in their natural environments."

After studying architecture at the Polytechnic Institute of Milan, Gabriele Basilico devoted himself to professional photography. Reports on construction projects and architecture were his principal assignments of that period. Various book projects and publications followed in the years 1983 to 1987. His book "Porti di Mare" is particularly well-known, for which he received an international award at the 1990 "Mois de la Photo" in Paris.

With the photographs shown here, Gabriele Basilico presents us with perfect black-and-white photography, both in terms of photography with a large format camera as well as in terms of producing perfect prints from the original images. "For me, black-and-white photography is a powerful means of expression," says Gabriele Basilico, "because the conversion of natural colors into the finest tonal values makes it a vital creative element". His photographs also thrive on strong contrasts, at which this photographer is a virtuoso, using them almost like a means to create a subtle mood.

The language of black-and-white photography has its own fascination. It records colors and contrasts differently from the way our eyes perceive them, and with the conversion of colors into light and shade values it presents us with an unaccustomed but typically photographic image. It transplants us into an unreal world by not reproducing the subject in its natural colors but slightly altered and almost abstract. Perhaps it is this very abstractness that elicits an unusual fascination from the viewer; an abstraction that can be pleasant and beautiful, but that can also harshly exaggerate, accuse and dramatize. That gives black-and-white photography its own mode of expression, namely contrast, which can be

manipulated effectively and at will with filters at the time the original picture is taken and again during enlargement by the choice of gradation.

Gabriele Basilico is a consummate master of black-and-white technique. The originals that were submitted for reproduction in this book were superb quality prints on baryta paper with a broad range of tonal values and a richness in detail that served as an ideal vehicle for the photographer's pictorial expression. Basilico thus enriched the pictorial selection of these portfolios and he proved that black-and-white very much continues to be a powerful means of expression in architectural photography.

Waltraud Krase

"I want my photographs to document architecture as it is, without embellishing anything. I am particularly fond of modern structures, because they allow me great creative latitude."

Waltraud Krase, completed her training at the Bavarian State Institute for Photography in Munich and is a member of the German Association of Freelance Photographers (BFF). Some years ago, whilst in Frankfurt, she decided to specialize in architectural and interior photography. She has been working in many Europaen countries, but mostly in Germany. She has also performed many photographic assignments in the United States and in Japan.

Waltraud Krase enjoys an unconventional way of working: while photographic assignments for architects and for architectural magazines are in the forefront, she also independently practices her own artistic photography of architectural subjects, which gives her the freedom to implement her own ideas and objectives in the form of impressive photographs. "It often happens", comments Waltraud Krase, "that the architects or the clients end up selecting my photographs over those that they commissioned me to produce with very specific concepts ..."

This photographer has had years of experience and she is as much in love with architecture as she is with photography itself. Modern buildings in particular, are her domain, because their avant-garde elements correspond most appropriately to her sense of form and to her creative ideas. That is why she has been working for years on a fascinating pictorial documentation of modern museum buildings, very effectively using her own special pictorial language to describe the often unconventional architecture with its interesting elements of form. Add to this a flair for aesthetic pictorial composition, often complemented by the good luck of finding the scene flooded in a fantastic, moody light, which Waltraud Krase knows how to exploit with great expertise to create magnificent photographs. To the viewers, her pictures seem to be alive, as if the buildings could speak ...

"The most important factor in architectural photography is the light", states Waltraud Krase. "Light lends architectural elements their form and emphasizes the individual structures of façades and planes. Light makes colors glow and it creates contrasts". Waltraud Krase loves contrasts. Contrasts that serve her pictorial concepts, but also contrasts as creative elements for segregating and emphasizing pictorial elements.

Waltraud Krase works with a Sinar f and prefers lenses with the focal lengths of 47, 65, 75 and 135 mm. She uses these extreme wide-angle lenses almost exclusively with the 6 x 9 cm Sinar Rollfilm Holder. Advantage: access to a wide selection of films that are available most everywhere; it also eliminates the problem of reloading sheet film holders on the road. Furthermore, she can use the image circles of these lenses to better advantage at extreme camera adjustments by using the smaller picture format. Her favorite films are Kodak Ektachrome EPR for color transparencies and Kodak T-Max 100 for her black-and-white photographs.

Hans Georg Esch

Niedrichstrasse 34, D-50668 Cologne 1
Phone: (0221) 12 11 16, Fax: (0221) 13 47 60

 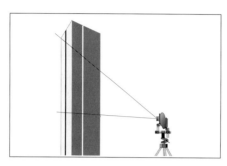

Subject:	**Frankfurt, Trade Fair Tower**
Camera - Objectiv:	**Sinar p2, 4 x 5" - Super-Angulon 1:5,6/90 mm**
Camera position:	**low**
Movements:	**front standard moved 5 cm upwards**
Aperture - Time:	**22 - $^{1}/_{60}$ s**
Remarks:	**A powerful dynamic effect was achieved by an extremely low camera position and by a strong shift of the front standard.**
Reference:	**Basics and applications, Practical exemple 1**

 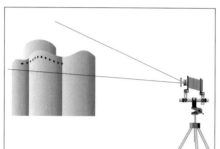

Subject:	**Düsseldorf, Theater**
Camera - Objectiv:	**Sinar p2, 4 x 5" - Sinaron W 1:6,8/155 mm**
Camera position:	**approx. 1,5 m**
Movements:	**front standard moved 4 cm upwards**
Aperture - Time:	**16 - $^{1}/_{30}$ s**
Remarks:	**The dramatic dark sky in this black-and-white image was achieved with the use of a red filter.**
Reference:	**Basics and applications, Practical exemple 1, Chapter 6.1.4**

 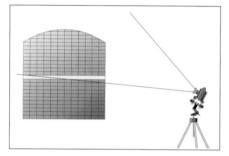

Subject:	**Frankfurt Trade Fair, Hall 9**
Camera - Objectiv:	**Sinar p2, 4 x 5" - Super-Angulon 1:5,6/90 mm**
Camera position:	**approx. 1,5 m**
Movements:	**no adjustments**
Aperture - Time:	**32 - $^{1}/_{8}$ s**
Remarks:	**The converging lines were used as a creative element. The use of a red filter produces a darker rendition of the sky (vapor trails).**
Reference:	**Basics and applications, Chapter 3 III. 57, Chapter 6.1.4**

 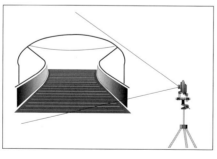

Subject:	**University of Zürich**
Camera - Objectiv:	**Sinar f, 4 x 5" - Grandagon N 1:6,8/75 mm**
Camera position:	**high, approx. 2 m**
Movements:	**front standard moved approx. 2 cm upwards**
Aperture - Time:	**22 - 4 s**
Remarks:	**A photograph with a pronounced central perspective. It is effective because of its complete symmetry. Vignetting in the dark portion of the subject is not critical.**
Reference:	**Basics and applications, Chap. 2.2, and 4.3.1**

 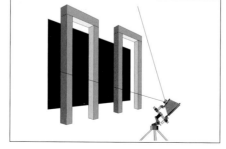

Subject:	**Residents and business buildings in Berlin**
Camera - Objectiv:	**Sinar p2, 8 x 10" - Sinaron W 1:6,8/155 mm**
Camera position:	**low**
Movements:	**sharpness compensation with front standard**
Aperture - Time:	**22 - 150 s**
Remarks:	**Dynamic perspective, obtained by not tilting rear standard. Strong variation of reproduction scale has the benefit of sharpness compensation.**
Reference:	**Basics and applications, Chapter 3 III. 57, Practical exemple 7**

Robert Polidori

85, rue de Turenne, F-75003 Paris
Phone/Fax: 01 - 48 87 42 92

 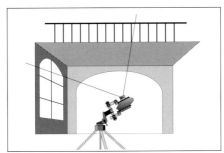

Subject: **Staircase in the Opera House in Palace of Versailles**
Camera - Objectiv: **Sinar p2, 4 x 5" - Grandagon N 1:4,5/75 mm**
Camera position: **extremly low**
Movements: **front standard moved 2 cm upwards**
Aperture - Time: **45 - 30 s**
Remarks: **Startling visual effect by extreme depth of field and dynamic pictorial composition. Time exposure on color negative film.**
Reference: **Basics and applications, Chapter 3, III. 57**

 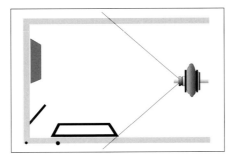

Subject: **First anteroom of Madame Victoire, Versailles**
Camera - Objectiv: **Sinar p2, 4 x 5" - Grandagon N 1:4,5/75 mm**
Camera position: **high, approx. 2 m**
Movements: **front standard 1 cm upwards**
Aperture - Time: **22 - 4 s**
Remarks: **The impression of spaciousness is conveyed effectively by the completely symmetrical composition and by the use of a wide-angle lens.**
Reference: **Basics and applications, Chapter 4.3.1 III. 72**

 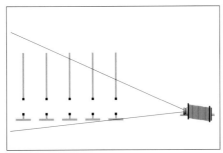

Subject: **17th Century Chambres in the Palace of Versailles**
Camera - Objectiv: **Sinar p2, 4 x 5"
Schneider Super Symmar HM 1:5,6/210 mm**
Camera position: **approx. 1,6 m**
Movements: **front standard 2 cm upwards and 3 cm to the right**
Aperture - Time: **32 - 12 s**
Remarks: **The strong visual effect of the receding door frames is created by central perspective and by a lateral shift of the front standard.**
Reference: **Basics and applications, Practical exemple 4**

 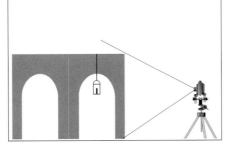

Subject: **Staircase in the Palace of Versailles**
Camera - Objectiv: **Sinar p2, 4 x 5" - Grandagon N 1:4,5/75 mm**
Camera position: **approx. 1,5 m**
Movements: **front standard moved 1,5 cm downwards and 1 cm to the left**
Aperture - Time: **32 - 60 s**
Remarks: **Daylight and a long exposure time called for color negative film type L and an 85B conversion filter. Caution: reciprocity failure!**
Reference: **Basics and applications, Chap. 5.1, Chap. 6.1.3**

 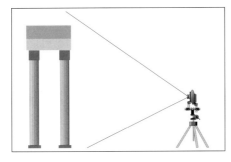

Subject: **Les Petites Ecuries, Palace of Versailles**
Camera - Objectiv: **Sinar p2, 4 x 5" - Grandagon N 1:4,5/75 mm**
Camera position: **1,5 m**
Movements: **front standard moved 2,5 cm upwards**
Aperture - Time: **32 - 10 s**
Remarks: **Polidori solves the problem of high contrast (1:64) by the use of color negative film and by enlargement on 8 x 10" print film.**
Reference: **Basics and applications, Chapter 5.4**

Reinhart Wolf

Bilderberg, Archiv der Fotografen GmbH
Hoheluftchausse 139, D-20253 Hamburg

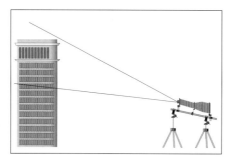

Subject: **Flatiron Building, New York**
Camera - Objectiv: **Sinar 8 x 10" - Apo Ronar MC 1:11/600 mm**
Camera position: **opposite building, approx. 10th floor**
Movements: **front standard upwards, back standard downwards**
Aperture - Time: **22 - $^1/_2$ s (morning twillight)**
Remarks: **The strong dynamic effect of this photograph was obtained by shifting the standards, harmonious cropping and parallel vertical lines.**
Remarks: **Basics and applications, Practical exemple 1**

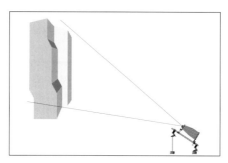

Subject: **United Nations Plaza, New York**
Camera - Objectiv: **Sinar 8 x 10" - Apo Ronar MC 1:9/360 mm**
Camera position: **relativly low**
Movements: **partially straightend. Front standard moved approx. 5 cm upwards**
Aperture - Time: **32 - $^1/_4$ s**
Remarks: **In order to emphasize the lateral extension of the structure, Wolf dispensed with the correction of verticals and with tight cropping.**
Reference: **Basics and applications, Practical exemple 3**

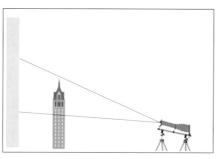

Subject: **Woolworth-Building and World Trade Center, New York**
Camera - Objectiv: **Sinar 8 x 10" - Apo Ronar MC 1:14/1000 mm**
Camera position: **high, opposite building**
Movements: **front standard moved approx. 4 cm upwards**
Aperture - Time: **32 - 6 s (twilight)**
Remarks: **This picture captures the viewer's attention with its architectural contrasts and with the perfect alignment of all vertical lines.**
Reference: **Basics and applications, Chap. 7.2 and 2.2 Fig 39**

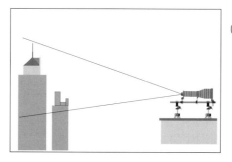

Subject: **Middle Building, Tudor City, New York**
Camera - Objectiv: **Sinar 8 x 10" - Apo Ronar MC 1:11/600 mm**
Camera position: **opposite building, approx. 25th floor**
Movements: **no adjustments**
Aperture - Time: **22 - 4 s, evening light**
Remarks: **Diffused light from an overcast sky produces good shadow detail in this photograph. Partially illuminated windows further enhance the image.**
Reference: **Basics and applications, Chapter 2.2 III. 39**

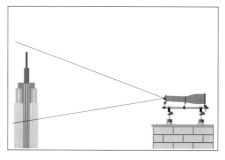

Subject: **Empire State Building, New York**
Camera - Objectiv: **Sinar 8 x 10" - Apo Ronar MC 1:14/1000 mm**
Camera position: **opposite building, approx. 25th floor**
Movements: **front standard moved approx. 4 cm upwards**
Aperture - Time: **16 - 4 s (morning twilight)**
Remarks: **The faint light of dawn and the background of an overcast sky show the world's tallest building in an eerie, nearly monochromatic mood.**
Reference: **Basics and applications, Chapter 7.2, Chapter 2.2 Fig 39**

Hardev Singh

L3 Green Park, New Delhi, 110 016, India
Phone: 011 - 662 046, Fax: 011 - 6 865 554

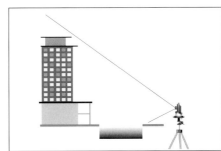

Subject: **Hotel Taj Man Singh, New Delhi**
Camera - Objectiv: **Sinar p2, 4 x 5" - Sinaron W 1:4,5/65 mm**
Camera position: **high, 3 to 4 m**
Movements: **front standard moved 1,5 cm upwards**
Aperture - Time: **22 - 3 s**
Remarks: **The combination of a high camera position, a wide-angle lens and strong shifts was used to straighten out converging lines. Caution: vignetting may have to be taken into account!**
Reference: **Basics and applications, Practical exemple 1**

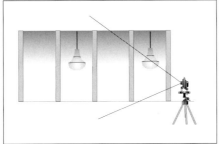

Subject: **Hotel The Mena House Oberoi, Kairo**
Camera - Objectiv: **Sinar p 4 x 5", Sinar zoom rollfilm holder format 6 x 7 cm - Sinaron W 1:6,8/75 mm**
Camera position: **approx. 1,5 m**
Movements: **front standard moved approx. 2 cm upwards**
Aperture - Time: **22 - 3 s**
Remarks: **Singh tolerates a minimal amount of background unsharpness. Even so, the viewer perceives the image to be sharp throughout.**
Reference: **Basics and applications, Chapter 4.5**

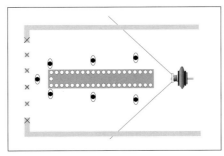

Subject: **Lake Palace, Udaipur, Indien**
Camera - Objectiv: **Sinar p, 4 x 5" - Sinaron W 1:4,5/65 mm**
Camera position: **approx. 1,5 m**
Movements: **front standard 4 cm upwards, sharpness compensation 2°**
Aperture - Time: **16 - 3 s**
Remarks: **Detailed art direction: every waiter is framed by an arched doorway. The photograph was made with available light and a conversion filter.**
Reference: **Basics and applications, Chapter 4.5**

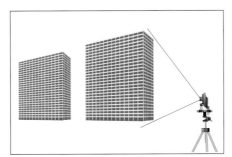

Subject: **Hotel Oberoi Towers, Bombay**
Camera - Objectiv: **Sinar p, 4 x 5" - Sinaron W 1:6,8/75 mm**
Camera position: **high, approx. 6 m**
Movements: **front standard moved 3 cm upwards**
Aperture - Time: **22 - 16 s**
Remarks: **The decrease in brightness ist caused simultaneously by the use of an extreme wide-angle lens and by twilight conditions.**
Reference: **Basics and applications, Practical exemple 1**

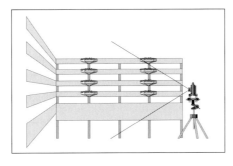

Subject: **Hotel Taj Bengal, Kalkutta**
Camera - Objectiv: **Sinar p2, 4 x 5" - Sinaron W 1:4,5/65 mm with centerfilter**
Camera position: **centered in front of the building**
Movements: **no adjustments**
Aperture - Time: **16 - 2,5 s**
Remarks: **This extreme wide-angle photograph shows a completely centered perspective. The normal drop-of in brightness requires a centerfilter.**
Reference: **Basics and applications, Chapter 4.3.1 Fig 72**

Chris Gascoigne

17a Harefield Road, London N8 8QY
Phone: 081 - 348 5279, Fax: 081 - 342 8719

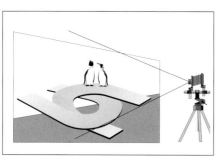

Subject: **Regent Park Zoo, London**
Camera - Objectiv: **Sinar f2, 4 x 5" - Sinaron W 1:6,8/115 mm**
Camera position: **high**
Movements: **front standard moved 4 cm downwards**
Aperture - Time: **32 - $^1/_{30}$ s**
Remarks: **By selecting the most appropriate camera position, the photographer was able to convey the interplay of forms in the design of the basin in the most effective manner.**
Reference: **Basics and applications, Chapter 4.3.1 Fig 73**

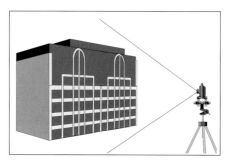

Subject: **Denison House, Victoria Station, London**
Camera - Objectiv: **Sinar p2, 4 x 5" - Sinaron W, 1:4,5/65 mm**
Camera position: **high, opposite building, approx. 8th floor**
Movements: **no adjustments**
Aperture - Time: **16 - $^1/_{100}$ s**
Remarks: **This photograph is successful because it was made at the perfect moment when ideal illumination of the façade coincided with dramatic cloud formations.**
Reference: **Basics and applications, Chapter 4.3.1 Fig 72**

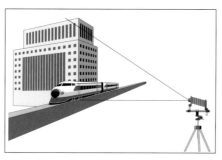

Subject: **Amex Building Canary Wharf, London**
Camera - Objectiv: **Sinar p2, 4 x 5" - Sinaron WS 1:5,6/300 mm**
Camera position: **high**
Movements: **front standard moved 8 cm upwards**
Aperture - Time: **16/22 - $^1/_{60}$ s**
Remarks: **The long focal length of the lens makes the building look huge to the viewer, and the moving train gives the picture additional vitality.**
Reference: **Basics and applications, Practical exemple 1**

Subject: **The Clore Gallery Extension, Tate Gallery, London**
Camera - Objectiv: **Sinar f2, 4 x 5" - Sinaron 1:4,5/90 mm**
Camera position: **high, approx. 2,5 m**
Movements: **front standard moved 3 cm upwards and 2 cm to the left**
Aperture - Time: **16 $^2/_3$ - $^1/_{60}$ s**
Remarks: **Avoiding reflections in glass façades often governs the selection of the best camera position.**
Reference: **Basics and applications, Practical exemple 5**

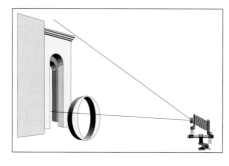

Subject: **Marco Polo/Observer Building, London**
Camera - Objectiv: **Sinar p2, 4 x 5" - Sinaron WS 1:5,6/210 mm**
Camera position: **high**
Movements: **front standard mouved 6 cm upwards and 2,5 cm to the left**
Aperture - Time: **22 - $^1/_{60}$ s**
Remarks: **This photograph is striking because of its ingenious composition looking at a moving train through the Oand through an archway.**
Reference: **Basics and applications, Practical exemple 4**

Gabriele Basilico

Piazza Tricolore 4, I-20129 Milano
Phone/Fax: 02 - 79 96 11

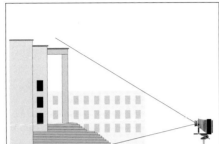

Subject: **"La Sapienza" University, Roma**
Camera - Objectiv: **Linhof Technika 4 x 5"**
Super-Angulon 1:5,6/90 mm
Camera position: **low**
Movements: **front standard moved 3 cm upwards**
Aperture - Time: **32 - $^1/_{100}$ s**
Remarks: **The high contrast range created by grazing light gives the façade of this building a three-dimensional effect.**
Reference: **Basics and applications, Chapter 5.4**

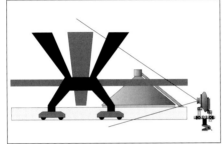

Subject: **Boulogne sur mer**
Camera - Objectiv: **Sinar f, 4 x 5" - Grandagon 1:8/90 mm**
Camera position: **low**
Movements: **front standard moved 4 cm upwards**
Aperture - Time: **22 - $^1/_{100}$ s**
Remarks: **Total back light and the featureless dominating conveyor lines give this picture its dramatic effect.**
Reference: **Basics and applications, Chapter 2.3 Fig 49, 50**

Subject: **Dunkerk**
Camera - Objectiv: **Sinar f, 4 x 5" Grandagon 1:6,8/90 mm**
Camera position: **low**
Movements: **front standard moved 3 cm upwards**
Aperture - Time: **11 - 60 s**
Remarks: **The static nature of a coal conveyor installation is suddenly transformed into a powerful document of industrial architecture.**
Reference: **Basics and applications, Practical exemple 13**

Subject: **Beach at Hardelot**
Camera - Objectiv: **Linhof Technika, 4 x 5"**
Super-Angulon 1:5,6/90 mm
Camera position: **low**
Movements: **front standard moved 3 cm upwards**
Aperture - Time: **22 - $^1/_{100}$ s**
Remarks: **Cloud formations enhanced by an yellow filter and the strong shadow in the foreground create a dynamic effect in this photograph.**
Reference: **Basics and applications, Chapter 6.1.4**

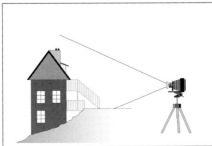

Subject: **Ault**
Camera - Objectiv: **Linhof Technika, 4 x 5"**
Super-Angulon 1:5,6/90 mm
Camera position: **approx. 2 m**
Movements: **no adjustments**
Aperture - Time: **22 - $^1/_{100}$ s**
Remarks: **The large proportion of the sky (dark yellow filter) in relation to the sea give the viewer an impression of infinite distance.**
Reference: **Basics and applications, Chapter 6.1.4**

Waltraud Krase

Gutleutstrasse 13, D-60329 Frankfurt 1
Phone: (069) 25 13 47, Fax: (069) 23 99 07

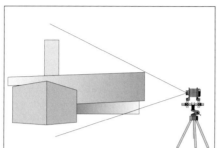

Subject:	**Museum of Design, Weil am Rhein**
Camera - Objectiv:	**Sinar f, 4 x 5", Sinar zoom rollfilm holder format 6 x 9 cm - Super-Angulon 1:5,6/47 mm**
Camera position:	**approx. 1,8 m**
Movements:	**no adjustments**
Aperture - Time:	**16 - 8 s**
Remarks:	**Twilight and the inclusion of existing light sources in this long exposure created a fascinating color effect.**
Reference:	**Basics and applications, Practical exemple 13**

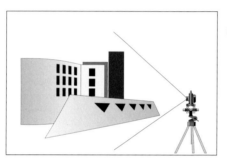

Subject:	**Company Braun, Melsungen**
Camera - Objectiv:	**Sinar f, 4 x 5", Sinar zoom rollfilm holder format 6 x 9 cm - Super-Angulon 1:5,6/47 mm**
Camera position:	**approx. 5 m**
Movements:	**no adjustments**
Aperture - Time:	**16 - $1/60$ s**
Remarks:	**Natural falling off of brightness in large, uniform areas (sky or sand) becomes noticeable when the most extreme wide-angle lenses are used.**
Reference:	**Basics and applications, Chapter 1.3**

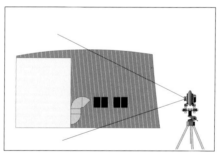

Subject:	**Company Braun, Melsungen**
Camera - Objectiv:	**Sinar f 4 x 5", Sinar zoom rollfilm holder format 6 x 9 cm - Grandagon 1:4,5/75 mm**
Camera position:	**approx. 2 m**
Movements:	**no adjustments**
Aperture - Time:	**16 - $1/60$ s**
Remarks:	**The impression of the right half of this picture is misleading: the "skewed" lines are caused by the slanted surface of the façade.**
Reference:	**Basics and applications, Practical exemple1**

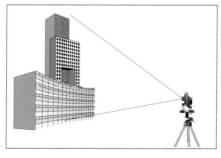

Subject:	**Tower building of the Frankfurt Trade Fair**
Camera - Objectiv:	**Sinar f, 4 x 5", Sinar zoom rollfilm holder format 6 x 9 cm - Grandagon 1:4,5/75 mm**
Camera position:	**high**
Movements:	**front standard moved 2 cm upwards**
Aperture - Time:	**16 - $1/60$ s**
Remarks:	**Waltraud Krase prefers high camera positions for her architectural photographs and adjusts the camera only to straighten out vertical lines.**
Reference:	**Basics and applications, Practical exemple 4**

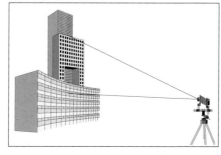

Subject:	**Tower building of the Frankfurt Trade Fair**
Camera - Objectiv:	**Sinar f, 4 x 5", Sinar zoom rollfilm holder format 6 x 9 cm - Symmar-S 1:5,6/135 mm**
Camera position:	**1,5 m**
Movements:	**front standard moved 2,5 cm upwards**
Aperture - Time:	**16 - $1/60$ s**
Remarks:	**Close-ups of architectural details are often more impressive and more significant than overall views.**
Reference:	**Basics and applications, Practical exemple 1**

Suggested Equipment Lists

The Mini-Outfit

	4 x 5"	5 x 7" / 13 x 18 cm	8 x 10"
Camera	Sinar f2	Sinar f2	Sinar f2
Lenses	Sinaron-W 1:4,5/90 mm DB Sinaron-W 1:6,8/155 mm DB	Sinaron-W 1:6,8/115 mm DB Sinaron-WS 1:5,6/210 mm DB	Sinaron-W 1:6,8/155 mm DB Sinaron-WS 1:5,6/300 mm DB
Shutter and Light Meter	Sinar/Copal Minolta IV or IVF Sinar Booster 1	Sinar/Copal Minolta IV or IVF Sinar Booster 1	Sinar/Copal Minolta IV or IVF Sinar Booster 1
Accessories	Wide-angle bellows Jointed rod and bellows holder Universal bellows Filter holder 100 + Polarizing Filter Sinar magnifier Tripod with pan-tilt head 4 x 5" sheet film holders Sinar zoom rollfilm holder Camera case	Wide-angle bellows Jointed rod and bellows holder Universal bellows Filter holder 100 + Polarizing Filter Sinar magnifier Tripod with pan-tilt head 5 x 7" sheet film holders Camera case	Wide-angle bellows Jointed rod and bellows holder Universal bellows Filter holder 100 + Polarizing Filter Sinar magnifier Tripod with pan-tilt head 8 x 10" sheet film holders Camera case

The Midi-Outfit (Consists of the Mini-Outfit plus following additional equipment:)

	4 x 5"	5 x 7" / 13 x 18 cm	8 x 10"
Camera	Possibly Sinar p2 instead of Sinar f2	Possibly Sinar p2 instead of Sinar f2	Possibly Sinar p2 instead of Sinar f2
Lenses	Sinaron-W 1:4,5/75 mm DB Sinaron•W 6,8/115 mm DB Sianron-WS 1:5,6/210 mm	Sinaron-W 1:6,8/155 mm DB Sinaron-WS 1:5,6/300 mm DB	Sinaron-WS 1:5,6/210 mm DB Sinaron-S 1:9/480 mm DB
Shutter and Light Meter	Sinar/Copal Minolta IV or IVF Sinar Booster 1	Sinar/Copal Minolta IV or IVF Sinar Booster 1	Sinar/Copal Minolta IV or IVF Sinar Booster 1
Accessories	Multipurpose standard Bellows rod Bellows hood mask 2 Binocular magnifier, Binocular hood Set of Sinar Color Control Filters 100 Sinar Color Control Graduated Filter	Multipurpose standard Bellows rod Bellows hood mask 2 Binocular magnifier, Binocular hood Set of Sinar Color Control Filters 100 Sinar Color Control Graduated Filter	Multipurpose standard Bellows rod Bellows hood mask 2 Binocular magnifier, Binocular hood Set of Sinar Color Control Filters 100 Sinar Color Control Graduated Filter

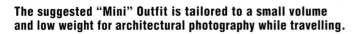

The suggested "Mini" Outfit is tailored to a small volume and low weight for architectural photography while travelling.

The expanded "Midi" Outfit provides the photographer with increased capability, but it is also slightly larger.

The Maxi-Outfit (Consists of the Midi-Outfit plus following additional equipment:)		
	4 x 5"	5 x 7" / 13 x 18 cm	8 x 10"
Camera	**Sinar p2 instead of Sinar f2**	**Sinar p2 instead of Sinar f2**	**Sinar p2 instead of Sinar f2**
Lenses	**Sinaron-W 1:4,5/65 mm DB** **Sinaron-WS 1:5,6/300 mm DB**	**Sinaron-S 1:9/480 mm DB**	**Apo-Sinaron 1:9/600 mm**
Shutter and Light Meter	**Sinar expolux System**	**Sinar expolux System**	**Sinar expolux System**
Accessories	**Binocular reflex magnifier** **Filter holder 125** **Set of Sinar Color Control Filters 125** **Graduated, Special Effect and** ** Polarizing Filters** **Sinar Black Box for loading Film** ** holders**	**Binocular reflex magnifier** **Filter holder 125** **Set of Sinar Color Control Filters 125** **Graduated, Special Effect and** ** Polarizing Filters** **Sinar Black Box for loading Film** ** holders**	**Binocular reflex magnifier** **Filter holder 125** **Set of Sinar Color Control Filters 125** **Graduated, Special Effect and** ** Polarizing Filters** **Sinar Black Box for loading Film** ** holders**

The "Maxi" Outfit offers the photographer virtually unlimited creative and photographic capabilities.